THE GURU OF JOY

THE GURU OF JOY
Sri Sri Ravi Shankar
&
The Art of Living

François Gautier

HAY HOUSE INDIA
Australia • Canada • Hong Kong
South Africa • United Kingdom • United States

Hay House Publications (India) Pvt. Ltd.
Muskaan Complex, Plot No.3, B-2 Vasant Kunj, New Delhi 110 070, India
Hay House Inc., PO Box 5100, Carlsbad, CA 92018-5100, USA
Hay House UK, Ltd., 292-B Kensal Rd., London W10 5BE, UK
Hay House Australia Pty Ltd., 18/36 Ralph St., Alexandria NSW 2015, Australia
Hay House SA (Pty) Ltd., PO Box 990, Witkoppen 2068, South Africa
Hay House Publishing, Ltd., 17/F, One Hysan Ave., Causeway Bay, Hong Kong
Raincoast, 9050 Shaughnessy St., Vancouver, BC V6P 6E5, Canada

ISBN 978-81-905655-9-2

Typeset in 11.5/13.5 Calisto by
Nikita Overseas Pvt. Ltd.

Printed and bound at
Thomson Press (India) Ltd

To
All gurus
present, past, and future

Contents

Foreword   9

Preface   11

Prologue: A Boat Ride in Banaras   15

1. A Sceptic's Tryst with Serenity   17

2. Glimpses of Childhood   33

3. The Celebration That Is Silence   45

4. The Days with Maharishi   55

5. The Way It All Began   61

6. From Student to Teacher   73

7. The Frame That Holds the Picture   95

8. The Steps That Speak   123

9. The Disciples   143

10. The Miracles   157

11. The Search for Scientific Proof   173

12. Sri Sri's Answers for the World Today   187

13. The Knowledge Sheets   209
14. A Glimpse into Eternity   221

Appendix 1   *225*
Appendix 2   *232*
References (Medical)   *235*

Foreword

At a time when many people feel that modern knowledge and ancient traditions tend to contradict each other, it is refreshing to come across someone like Sri Sri Ravi Shankar who has been able to reconcile his scientific education with his Vedic training to find a path relevant to contemporary needs. As a result, he has established the Art of Living Foundation, whose avowed aim of encouraging people from all backgrounds, religions, and cultural traditions to join together in celebration and service is highly admirable. I have had the pleasure of meeting him several times as well as visiting his ashram.

François Gautier's long-standing personal and professional interest in India has found expression in this book about Sri Sri Ravi Shankar. I am sure readers who are concerned to find ways to reawaken human values in their own lives today will find much here to inspire them.

– H. H. The Dalai Lama

Preface

Peace has many more meanings than we may think, and its absence in our lives produces more problems than we know. No one in the twenty-first century has probably worked more towards the promotion of peace than His Holiness Sri Sri Ravi Shankar. In recognition of his extraordinary achievements in this field, Sri Sri Ravi Shankar was nominated for the 2005 Nobel Peace Prize.

Who doesn't want a little peace of mind? In today's scenario, this entity appears to be something of a rarity. The daily stresses of modern living are taking a heavy toll physically and mentally, leading to conflict and friction at the workplace, nervous disorders, disease, and even suicide. The Art of Living course, created by His Holiness Sri Sri Ravi Shankar, provides tools that help in bringing back peace to our lives. Techniques in breathing, sound relaxation, and meditation, among many others, are used to eliminate stress from the system, so that the mind gains the clarity to look within and the body is able to calm and strengthen itself.

Today, even our children are subjected to a host of stresses, from broken homes and pressures at school to increasing exposure to violence and sex. Sri Sri Ravi Shankar thus came up with ART Excel (All Round Training in Excellence), a programme specifically designed for young people. This unique course promotes the understanding of human values and encourages the overall well-being of children and young adults through a variety of empowering techniques that foster mental clarity and focus, physical relaxation and health, and emotional stability.

We need peace in our society. Many of those who disturb that peace end up in jail, where they are meant to be reformed. But we know that, in reality, what happens is quite different: jails more often breed bitterness and anger towards society rather than bring about change. In view of this serious drawback, the Art of Living Foundation developed a programme called Prison SMART – Prison Stress Management and Rehabilitation Training. Aside from helping prisoners rehabilitate themselves, the programme teaches them life skills that enable inmates to accept responsibility for their past actions and to handle future conflicts successfully. In India, more than 120,000 prisoners from across the country have undergone Prison SMART with spectacular results. Now, it is being used in many jails around the world.

Terrorism is possibly the biggest threat to world peace today. Many political leaders believe they can counter terrorism only through war or other violent measures. But Sri Sri Ravi Shankar has understood that spirituality alone can vanquish terrorism. His special programmes have won over an Al-Qaeda terrorist from Bombay, Naxalites (leftist militants) from southern India, and over 50 terrorists from Kashmir prisons.

What about those who have been terrorized in different countries of the world? Eighty per cent of Kosovo's (a part of the former Yugoslavia that witnessed a great deal of violence from the 1980s onwards) population, for instance, suffers from post-traumatic stress disorder, according to the Harvard Medical Group. Art of Living volunteers have spent ten years working in Kosovo; later, they have been active in

Israel, other Balkan regions, Sudan, Afghanistan, Kashmir, Pakistan and, most recently, in war-ravaged Iraq, where people are beginning to successfully use yoga, meditation, and breathing techniques to overcome emotional and physical trauma.

Next, we come across those who have been affected by natural calamities, such as the 26 December 2004 tsunami that devastated many regions of Asia, apart from taking a heavy toll. About 5000 Art of Living volunteers were involved in tsunami relief efforts worldwide. Over 3500 people were treated for post-traumatic stress disorders by using a range of Art of Living methods. Hurricane Katrina, in August 2005, left a trail of destruction through Louisiana, Mississippi, and Alabama in the US. Victims immediately needed not only medical treatment, food, and water, but also the most urgent trauma care, which the Art of Living trauma relief programmes provided post-haste.

Finally, how will we ever attain peace if the poor and the downtrodden around the world are not looked after (and their agonies alleviated) and the divide between the haves and the have-nots isn't addressed? The 5H programme – home, health, hygiene, harmony in diversity, and human values – is helping to make a difference to the world through service and spirituality. The aim of this programme is to uplift individuals and communities so that they become self-reliant, socially and economically. Sri Sri Ravi Shankar's 'soldiers of peace' have adopted 25,300 Indian villages in 25 states, trained 25,710 village youngsters in youth leadership training programmes, and conducted over 75,000 village-oriented courses that have benefited more than 2.3 million people.

Sri Sri Ravi Shankar has touched the lives of numerous

people across the globe. In February 2006, 3.5 million people from 145 countries, including heads of state, religious leaders, and dignitaries, graced the silver jubilee celebrations of the Art of Living Foundation held in Bangalore. People from every race, religion, and creed came together to celebrate Sri Sri Ravi Shankar's message of peace, unity, and human understanding.

The Guru of Joy recounts the story of the true Apostle of Peace of the twenty-first century.

François Gautier

Prologue
A Boat Ride in Banaras

It was a beautiful November night, cool without being chilly. Two lean oarsmen had paddled us to the middle of the river Ganges (called Ganga in India) and then let the boat slowly drift with the current. A light mist made the faraway lights sparkle. The pilgrimage town of Kashi (in Uttar Pradesh; also known as Banaras or Varanasi) was already asleep and except for a few sadhus huddled around a makeshift fire, nobody else was visible on the banks. The silence, broken only by the soft lapping of water, was absolute, pregnant with a presence. At 9 p.m., the moon rose on the horizon, adorning the river in silver.

Sri Sri Ravi Shankar was sitting at the bow, draped in white robes, an enigmatic smile on his face. Then, one of the devotees quietly started humming a bhajan as ancient as the city of Kashi itself: 'Om namah Shivaya, Om namah Shivaya.' Soon all of us joined him, singing softly so as not to break the magic spell of the hushed silver night. After a moment, Sri Sri closed his eyes and, seeing him totally absorbed, perhaps in some mystical realm, touched our souls as nothing else could. An atmosphere of stillness and serenity descended on us. In a corner, a girl started shedding quiet tears of ecstasy; an elderly man joined his hands in a silent prayer, a wordless gesture of deeply felt gratitude. Everyone shone with intense inner joy, bliss, and wonder. As for me, to my surprise, I realized that the characteristic chattering in my mind had quietened; my soul soared high in the air. Perfectly in the moment, I savoured every bit of it.

Later, as we were driving back to the hotel, and I was holding this precious experience close to my heart, trying not to let it go, I tried to remember when and how it had all started.

Chapter One

A Sceptic's Tryst with Serenity

Meditation is seeing GOD in yourself
Love is seeing GOD in the person next to you
Knowledge is seeing GOD everywhere.

One morning, as I was sitting in the garden of my home in Auroville (a city based on Sri Aurobindo's vision that lies within Pondicherry, now called Puducherry, on South India's eastern coast) having a cup of tea with my wife Namrita, our friend Krishnakant from Paris unexpectedly visited us. This was his first trip to India after almost five years. An ardent devotee of Sri Aurobindo and the Mother, Krishnakant was keen to know all that had happened in the ashram and Auroville during his absence. We were discussing Sri Aurobindo's vision of enlightenment and the supramental, when, in the course of our conversation, I had one of my standard sneezing attacks. Casually, he said: 'Why don't you go to the Art of Living Centre in Bangalore and learn some breathing techniques? It might help.' He then gave me the address of the centre, which I reluctantly took and then completely forgot about.

I was cynical and sceptical because I had been living with this condition since I was six years old, when I was hit on my nose by a heavy steel swing at a fair. The impact had badly damaged the inner bone and impaired my breathing, and subsequent operations had not helped. Yet, a few months later, I actually thought about what Krishnakant had said; I thought I ought to check it out, but once again my logical mind dissuaded me.

At the time, I was writing for *Le Figaro*, France's largest circulated newspaper. Often, while working on the computer, I had noticed that my breathing had become shallow and I knew that it could only have negative effects on my body in the long run. Finally, I decided to take the plunge and go to Bangalore with Namrita. Perhaps if I did it, I thought, giving the cause added justification, some important shift might take place in my life and it would rekindle in me the intense spiritual aspiration and innocence I had known during my first years in Pondicherry, when the Mother was still there in Her body.

The next day, Namrita joined me on a flight to Bangalore. We took a taxi from the airport to Gyan Mandir, the Art of Living Centre in Bangalore city. In the car, I was lost in my thoughts, lamenting the state of affairs at work. I wondered whether my editor at *Le Figaro* would accept the story I had just submitted. I silently concluded that all this talk about freedom of the press was humbug. Where was the freedom? I was jolted out of my thoughts by a sudden scream from Namrita. A dog had darted across the road bringing our speeding car to a halt. The driver turned back with a smile, as though to reassure us that everything was under control! He then continued driving in a relaxed manner as if nothing had happened. To calm down a visibly shaken Namrita, I joked that these drivers played a dual role. They were not only there to chauffeur us around, but also sent to remind us to pray. And they certainly did a better job of it than the Catholic priests back home in France, I added.

Observing the driver, who still had a smile on his face and was now humming a tune, I wondered how he could be so relaxed in the midst of all this chaos, where neither law nor logic operated. These illiterate people seemed to have more faith than I, I thought. As I was comparing myself with the people around me, the driver again stopped and exchanged a few words in the local language with a passer-by. I got the impression that he was asking for directions apart from indulging in a bit of banter. I admired the friendliness between them and the jokes they were obviously enjoying – it was an easiness I had not experienced before. We rarely saw such camaraderie in France, I thought. Have we become too serious? No one encourages us to laugh and have fun – there went my mind galloping once again.

The car stopped once more, this time at our destination.

As it happened, an Art of Living Basic Course was about to start. Without much thought we enrolled ourselves for this course. As we entered the venue for the course, I glanced at Namrita, who comes from a rather Westernized Indian family, and knew that she was not in the least bit interested. Her path was set, as was her mind. She was doing this only because I had persuaded her to. Our instructor, Michael Fischman, an American, began to speak: 'We all want happiness, love, and peace. We fail to realize this because we are stressed. The breathing techniques that we learn here will help to release stress.' He went on to explain the laws that govern the seven layers of our existence (just as the earth is comprised of seven layers) and the four sources of energy (physical capacity, emotional resilience, mental endurance, and spiritual flexibility).

As the course progressed, it kindled my interest. I turned around and looked at my wife. Her reluctance seemed to be easing. I observed the others in the group. They all seemed to be absorbed in Michael's explanations; they evidently wanted to understand the simple truths of their own lives. My rebellious journalistic mind, however, was still analysing and questioning everything. But Michael was calmness personified, and seldom put me down. I admired his patience in fielding all sorts of questions from this motley bunch. Perhaps, if I had been him, I thought, I would have lost my temper. I wondered what made him remain so poised. Even though what he said made sense, I continued to have misgivings. At the end of the session, as we were walking out of the venue, Arvind, one of the participants, said: 'You know, I'm an agnostic, but today, something about the teaching – and the man behind the teaching – has touched me deeply. I have decided to proceed with this course, even though I came here against my will, only because my wife forced me to.' This declaration moved us: if an agnostic, a man who had been a total sceptic, as he had confessed to us, could be touched by these simple 'basic' techniques, then maybe there was something more to Art of Living than we thought. Namrita and I also decided to come back the next day.

And so it was that we found ourselves again in Gyan Mandir the next evening, a little more receptive than we had been on the previous day. However, immediately upon starting the session, Michael gently urged Namrita, who was still holding back, 'to give her 100 per cent'. She got upset and began thinking: What does this man know? I have practised many forms of pranayama (breath control; literally means 'suspension of breath') before in Auroville. As she was fretting and fuming, she suddenly became aware that the pattern of her breathing had changed: it had become shorter and more laboured. It then dawned on her that the breath is indeed the connecting link between the mind and emotions; that when one is anxious, under pressure, or stressed, there is a deviation from the natural rhythm of breathing. With this realization something opened up in her and she decided to commit herself to whatever was to come. And then we experienced the Sudarshan Kriya (a unique rhythmical breathing process that is said to have been revealed to Sri Sri Ravi Shankar during a spell of silent meditation that he had undertaken for 10 days in 1982). This experience was so powerful that it literally blew my mind. For the first time since I could remember, I became quiet and serene. It was like taking a holiday from my chaotic mind; it was an unusually calm state. Suddenly, I felt that all the trouble we had taken in coming all this way had been worth it.

As the days went by, we grew closer as a group and began feeling benevolent even towards those who had irritated us no end at the start. Like Vijay, for instance, who had an annoying habit of nibbling snacks all the time. Michael, however, never commented on this habit, nor did he show any impatience, and his compassion and serenity went a long way in helping us to realize how far we had to go. Michael made us see how we were boxed in within our small judgemental minds, which were constantly scrutinizing things and people, accepting some, rejecting most. Without quite realizing it, we were beginning to imbibe one of the most important lessons in life: To accept people as they are. We grew to understand that these lessons, which appear so simple, are actually 'sutras', secrets of a well-lived life. (Sutra can also mean a spiritual narrative.)

When it was time to leave, we all got up and greeted each other, as we had begun, by saying, 'I belong to you'. And oh, how different it felt this time! Indeed, we actually felt that we had come to belong to each other, and that, in these six days, there had grown a beautiful and touching bond between people who were not long ago strangers to one other. Namrita and I looked at each other and realized that something had changed within us too; we had become lighter, freer from within. It felt as though we had taken a new birth. We had heard about the 'born-again experience', but till then those had been just words. Now we felt that we had become children again at heart, free and loving.

On our way back to Auroville, we were standing on the railway platform, and there were ten minutes left for the train to arrive. Usually, the wait would have made us restless, but this time it did not. And then there was the signal: the train had arrived – to take us on the journey towards a new beginning.

We went back to Auroville, but the memories of the Art of Living Basic Course remained with us and we continued practising the techniques we had learnt. I noticed a significant change in myself. I was not the same person. Suddenly, life around me had become much more vibrant. I wondered whether this was a temporary euphoric state. I wanted to know more. And persistently, one thought kept nagging me: Who is Sri Sri? Until then I had only heard about him. Who was this man, I caught myself wondering, who had devised this incredibly beautiful and powerful course? I had to see him. Perhaps this curiosity drove me to call up the Bangalore ashram. I was told about the Advanced Course and I signed up for it right away. Namrita chose to stay back.

I went back to Bangalore and drove straight to the ashram, which is about 20 km outside the city. 'An ashram is a place where one comes to rest: *a-shram*, to come home and let go of all your worries,' says Sri Sri. (Shram means work or labour.) Although I had no dispute with that interpretation, the human mind is such that one instinctively resists changing one's surroundings, getting out of one's routine, giving up one's habits, and being thrown into a new environment. I felt apprehensive as I approached the ashram.

The atmosphere at this ashram did not reflect the 'spirituality' I was familiar with. People here smiled and laughed. A mood of celebration permeated the place. The hills, the greenery, and the lake situated at the other end of the compound – everything was so beautiful. The chirping of birds and insects in the stillness of an autumn evening imbued the place with a magical ambience. In the ashram everyone is required to do two hours of seva (selfless service) – be it chopping vegetables, translating various publications, transcribing books and speeches, gardening, cleaning the floor, and so on. Though groups of people were engaged in various such activities, there was laughter and joy everywhere – entirely contrary to my concept of spiritual and religious places as being quiet and serious. A sense of celebration crept into me too. I went around asking what I could do. As I was one of the few Westerners there, they gave me some 'light work': pruning a bush and watering a few pots. As I began to do this work, I felt a surge of enthusiasm. I wanted to do this little job perfectly. Perhaps this is what Sri Sri meant by living in the moment and really enjoying it.

I had the privilege of doing my first Advanced Course with Rajshree Patel and Philip. Rajshree was a thin and intense-looking Indian American. She was a patient, soft-spoken and compassionate teacher, but one could often sense a fire within her. We owe her so much for the solid grounding she gave us in the techniques that we have practised ever since. She was also, like all the senior teachers, totally, entirely, and wholeheartedly devoted to Sri Sri. If Rajshree was all fire, Philip was the soft, gentle face of their partnership. Always smiling, ever helpful, perpetually dressed in white kurta and pyjamas, his hair (which was long and black at the time) carefully combed back, Philip was a professional American musician, who had met Guruji by chance and stayed with him ever since. Never asserting himself, never raising his voice, he also seemed to be a born teacher. He would always be the first one up in the morning, and we would awake to the melodious sound of his flute. By the time we reached the hall, sleepy and bleary-eyed, he would already be seated there with his eyes closed, looking serene and rested, although he would probably not have slept more than a few hours at night. In fact, it is through Philip that we understood the concept of seva, selfless work. Most of the teachers at the ashram didn't keep track of the time and energy spent on work, and would not give a thought to a skipped meal or a sleepless night in the service of their Guru. Theirs was a great frame of mind and the key to forgetting oneself.

In fact, it was their sense of commitment, coupled with their humility, which moved me the most. I started comparing my editor at *Le Figaro* with them. If only my editor was half as considerate and patient as these people, I could do so much more. Then a thought struck me – why don't they teach these techniques to corporate people and journalists? I would convey this thought to Sri Sri when I meet him, I decided. I thought I was giving him a new idea. I was sure that this was what the world really needed today – an atmosphere marked by an easygoing attitude and a sense of celebration, in which one would not lose one's commitment to the work undertaken and would gain perfection without being subject to stress. Sitting down by the bush I was trimming, I quickly took a notepad from my pocket to make some notes. Then I remembered what we had just been taught: to give 100 per cent to whatever we were doing. Realizing that I had lost sight of the task at hand, I put away my notepad and got back to my shears. My Advanced Course had truly begun!

As part of the course, we maintained a few days of silence. In the words of Sri Sri Ravi Shankar: 'The practice of silence has been known throughout the ages, in many different traditions and cultures, as a great tool for enhancing self-discovery. Maintaining silence, even for just a few days, can have remarkable effects on the system, reviving energy and enthusiasm, and providing deep rest for the mind and body.' Though I had done a Vipassana course earlier, this silence was different. I now realized that silence and joy could go hand in hand, and that being in a state of silence need not make you grim or sombre.

Meditation was another vital component of the course. Even though I had learnt meditation, Sri Sri's opening sentence – 'Meditation is not concentration, it is de-concentration' – made me sit up. This was the introduction to Sri Sri's unique 'hollow and empty meditation'. Philip developed this concept further: 'We gain so much from our efforts in life, yet there are some things that effort cannot accomplish. Meditating is the delicate art of doing nothing – letting go of everything and being who you are. It allows the conscious mind to settle deeply into itself; and when the mind settles down, it lets go of all tension and stress and centres itself in the present moment. Regular practice of meditation, once or twice a day, can totally transform the quality of your life.'

Every evening we attended a satsang, an assembly where everyone sang hymns to the Divine in His different manifestations. Satsang was an integral part of the Advanced Course. 'The whole day you make efforts, concentrate, use your mind, strive,' Rajshree had told us, 'but during satsang, you let go of everything and just be in the togetherness of your hearts.'

When we entered the meditation hall for our first satsang, Sri Sri Ravi Shankar, who had just come back from a trip abroad, was already seated on the dais, eyes closed, in deep meditation. At first, I cannot say that I felt a tremendous revelation in his presence, but I remembered Sri Aurobindo's words: 'Even if the Divine were to manifest Himself in front of you in His full glory, you would not recognize Him.' After some time, though, I did begin to feel a glow in my heart: something was happening there; I started feeling a presence, an acknowledgement of something wonderful happening.

By then, the satsang was in full swing. I had never attended one before in my entire life and do not care much for singing. But suddenly, it seemed to me that I recognized these marvellous hymns being sung in a foreign tongue, by people from a different culture: these were my people, these were my songs, which I had hummed before, though I didn't know where and how! All my fellow course participants were glowing. All had smiles on their faces – some seemed to be in a state of ecstasy, their eyes closed, bodies swinging, hands clapping; others had gone into quiet and intense meditation, immobile but relaxed. Sri Sri's eyes were still closed, but there exuded from him such an intense feeling of concentrated silence, of deep meditation, and of emotionless bliss, that it carried us all away through cloudless skies. As I was gazing at him, he suddenly opened his eyes and looked straight at me, piercing my heart with an emotion I could not fathom. Once again the question sprang up in me: Who was this man?

As per the practice after every satsang, wherever in the world he may be, Sri Sri answered questions from the participants. I was surprised at the manner in which he tackled the most difficult questions – his were profound ideas expressed in a few simple words, almost making me believe that there was nothing to it. His answers were spontaneous and laced with wit. It seemed as if he didn't need to think to answer, and of course nothing could take his smile away. I noted down some of the exchanges that night:

Q: What happens after death?
Sri Sri: Let there be some suspense! I can assure you, you are not going to miss it. That's for sure!
Q: How can one improve patience?
Sri Sri: I will tell you that next year.
Q: How do I improve my memory?
To this question, Sri Sri remained silent for a while, dealt with other answers, and then came back to that person, saying: 'What was your question?'
Q: Do you love everyone equally?
Sri Sri: No, I love everyone uniquely!
Q: Why is it that you have so many followers?
Sri Sri: I don't turn my back on anyone, so how can I have followers?
Q: I'm an interior decorator...

Sri Sri: Oh, we do the same job!

Q: Do you ever get angry?

Sri Sri: I can, but it's very expensive. Make your smile cheap and anger expensive!

He laughed and then burst into the bhajan that usually concludes satsangs: 'Jai, Jai Radhe …'

The Advanced Course is also about understanding the bond you share with other people, whether they're strangers or people you know. By the end you discover how close you can feel to people who have existed outside your own little world; how all men and women are wonderful, if not perceptibly, at least deep inside, in their essence. Finally, you are made to realize that the art of living well is really all about letting go, dropping your unrealistic expectations and your hang-ups and allowing Sri Sri to take you step by step, like a mother leads her child by the hand, from tension to release, from ego to joy, from darkness to light. By themselves, seva, meditation, and satsang were simple concepts to follow and understand. But the way in which these concepts were combined and delivered in the Advanced Course was extremely powerful.

Soon, I felt a transformation inside me. And I was not alone. Similar transformations seemed to be taking place behind the shining faces of each of my co-participants. Speaking of Sri Sri, I have to admit that though I was so enamoured of his techniques, at the time, I still dissociated them from him and there was no question of surrendering myself to him: I had never bowed to anybody in my life and I was not going to start now. Still, the man fascinated me; his look during satsang had pierced my soul and I would observe him from the corner of my eye during sessions. And when he would cap the 'hollow and empty meditation' with his Sanskrit chanting of slokas, always ending with 'Om Shanti, Om Shanti, Om Shanti', my heart would leap and something in me would melt.

My desire to meet Sri Sri was fulfilled on the last day of the course. So simple and unpretentious, he asked me about my life, what I did, and where I was at that point of time. He did not try to pressurize me to come back or to become an Art of Living disciple. Yet, his presence conveyed so much love that when I came out, something had melted inside me. When I returned to Auroville and my wife saw me, radiant and glowing, happy and at peace, something in her also changed and whatever resistance she still had vanished. As for me, I could only describe my experience in three words: 'It was fantastic.'

We both had work commitments – she had a small children's cloth factory, I was working with *Le Figaro* – but we decided to go back together as soon as possible for another Advanced Course. At the beginning of 1995, we reached the ashram again: the smiling faces had become more familiar and Guruji greeted us with a radiant 'Jai Gurudev', as if he had always known we would return so fast. Yet again, we had a wonderful course, leading to a unique bonding together and with others. Namrita learnt the techniques that I had two months earlier and enjoyed them so much that we decided to return for the next Advanced Course too. In fact, we kept coming back, course after course, year after year – we must have done twelve Advanced Courses in four years. Slowly, we started letting go of some of our resistance towards the Guru, experiencing inside us the sweetness, the gratitude, and the love that all disciples throughout the ages have felt towards their gurus. He made it so easy for us, as for many others, never putting pressure on either of us, but always saying: 'This too is your home,' knowing fully well that we were disciples of Sri Aurobindo and the Mother and that Auroville was our base.

On my part, my mind still buzzed with questions: Who was this man? Where had he come from? What was our relationship to be with him? And was bowing to him a move that would force us to let go of our capacity to reason and choose, to analyse and discriminate? Was it not tantamount to surrendering our free will?

Chapter Two

Glimpses of Childhood

Stretching sound is music,
Stretching movement is dance,
Stretching the smile is laughter,
Stretching the mind is meditation,
Stretching life is celebration,
Stretching the devotee is GOD,
Stretching feeling is ecstasy,
Stretching emptiness is bliss.

The more you appreciate a person, the more you want to know about him or her. Who then is the real Sri Sri? There is very little that is known about him and, like many yogis, he is not very forthcoming about his personal life. One day I ventured to directly ask Guruji about himself: 'What did you want to be when you were growing up?' 'I was a child, I am a child, when did I grow up?' he answered with a twinkle in his eyes. Though I was pleased by his answer, I was not satisfied. It didn't help quench my journalistic curiosity. I felt he had just avoided the question. This is the problem with Eastern mystics, I thought: they don't like to talk much about themselves. Perhaps they think that such reticence displays humility. Most Indians, I concluded, never give enough importance to history or biography. I didn't understand the logic behind such humility.

I wanted to know more. This urge compelled me to meet Sri Sri's father, his aunt, his sister Bhanu, and some of his old associates, friends, and classmates. When I asked them about Sri Sri, their eyes would light up and they would smile. Transported back in time, they would go on for hours narrating their stories. Piecing them all together, here is what I learnt.

Sri Sri Ravi Shankar was born on 13 May 1956 in Papanasam, a village in Tamil Nadu in South India. Sri Sri's father, R. S. V. Ratnam (referred to as Pitaji), was Western educated and his thinking was modern and reformist in nature. His mother, Visalakshi (referred to as Amma), however, came from a traditional orthodox Brahmin family. There is a spiritual meaning to his name, as he came into the world on Shankara Jayanti, the birth anniversary of the great Indian reformer, Adi Shankara, who is believed to have lived the eighth century AD. He was thus named on the eleventh day of his birth, which was Ramanuja Jayanti, the day Ramanuja (another important theologian and Hindu philosopher who lived in the eleventh and twelfth century AD) was born. And as his native village was famous for its Shiva and Vishnu temples, his parents named him Ravi Shankar. It is only recently that 'Ravi' and 'Shankar' have sometimes been clubbed together into one word. Someone once asked him why he has two 'Sris' in his name. He is reported to have replied (with the characteristic twinkle in his eye): 'Because 108 Sris would make it too long.' (Usually, Hindu Gods and deities have 108 names each.)

Little Ravi Shankar showed remarkable devotional powers and it soon became apparent that he was a very special child. Various sources disclosed to me that Sri Sri could recite the Bhagavad Gita at a very young age. It appears that when Sri Sri was four, his parents took him to Thangamma, a Sanskrit teacher. She was a Gandhian and would conduct Sanskrit classes and satsangs every day. People from all religious backgrounds would come to learn from her. It is said that when the teacher started the first line 'Parthaaya Pratibodhitaam' and waited for little Ravi Shankar to repeat it, he chanted 'Bhagavataam Narayanena Swayum', thus completing the verse! She was astounded by the fact that a child could not only recite from an ancient sacred text when he couldn't read, but also that he could do so without having been taught to! When he was taken to the nearby school to begin his academic career, his teachers recognized his extraordinary intelligence, and he was given two double promotions. And so by the time he was seventeen, he had acquired a fair amount of knowledge of Vedic literature, had completed his traditional studies and secured a Bachelor's degree in modern science!

When young Ravi Shankar expressed further interest in learning Sanskrit, his parents arranged Pandit Sudakar Chaturvedi to teach him. The pandit had been Mahatma Gandhi's Sanskrit teacher as well as his secretary for South India. In fact, Sri Sri was the pandit's first pupil since the Mahatma. There is an interesting story behind this fact. During Partition (August 1947), the Mahatma was deeply pained. He was losing faith in all his close aides. When the news of Hindus and Muslims slaughtering each other reached him, he refused to believe it. To get a first-hand account, he sent Pandit Chaturvedi to Lahore (now in Pakistan). Upon reaching that city, the pandit saw that it was the Hindus who were being tortured and killed by the Muslims; he himself was attacked, stripped, beaten, stabbed several times, and buried up to the neck in a sand pit. He was saved in the nick of time by an army officer. When he narrated the scene, which sounded worse than a civil war to Gandhiji, the Mahatma refused to believe him, saying that he was prejudiced because he was a Hindu himself. Chaturvedi was deeply hurt that Gandhiji had lost faith in him. Upset and annoyed, he returned to Bangalore. Three days later (on 30 January 1948) the Mahatma was assassinated. Pandit Chaturvedi would share this story with everyone he met, ending with a note of regret about how he felt he had betrayed the Mahatma in his last days. In Bangalore, he wrote several books and gave discourses in the Arya Samaj (an organization founded by Swami Dayanand Saraswati in 1875 to propagate the Vedas, which has branches in various parts of India). He did not formally teach anyone till young Ravi Shankar came along.

Once, when he was five years old, an aged pandit, Samba Dixit, visited Guruji's house. Dixit brought out various deities and asked the boy to choose one of them. Ravi Shankar chose a Shiva lingam (an iconic representation of the God), made of emerald, and a silver serpent. Dixit was impressed and revealed that the lingam originally belonged to the family of Muthuswami Dikshitar (1775–1835) – a renowned saint and composer-singer of South India. He interpreted it as a sign that young Ravi Shankar would grow up to be an upholder of truth and righteousness (dharma).

As a young child, Ravi Shankar was a keen observer and rebellious by nature. He could not accept injustice in any form. When he was around nine years old, he had gone to his maternal grandmother's village for spending the summer vacation. Here he came across the practice of 'untouchability' for the first time. (Bangalore being a cosmopolitan city, he had not been exposed to this scourge there.) In the village, he loved playing with the cows and calves, and the man who would take care of them was a Harijan named Swaminathan. He observed that because Swaminathan was from a lower caste, he was not allowed to enter their home and even had to have his food outside the house. Young Sri Sri was not allowed to touch him and if he did he was punished and promptly made to bathe. Swaminathan may have resigned himself to this social order, but not young Ravi Shankar. This was unacceptable. He questioned his grandmother: 'Why do you treat him so?' Pat came the reply: 'He is an untouchable.' In response, Sri Sri would quote from the Bhagavad Gita: 'Ishvaro Sarvabhutanam ....' (God lives in every heart, in every human being). His words fell on deaf ears. But the rebel in him would not be subdued and he would first touch Swaminathan, then his grandmother, and then all her clothes that she had hung out to dry. She would not let anyone, not even her family members, touch her clothes, so when Sri Sri would go and pull all of them down, all hell would break loose! Morevoer, he would also share his food with Swaminathan's children. One day he took Swaminathan's bicycle to his house. This created such a storm in the family that the very next day his mother had to take him back to Bangalore.

In spite of their disagreements, Sri Sri was very close to his grandmother, and when he discovered that people died after they grew old, he became very anxious and was afraid of losing her. He would sleep with her and sit up all night watching her breathing. 'Every time I felt she was not breathing,' he recalls today, 'I would wake her up, and as long as she was snoring – which she did loudly – I was happy.' It was at that time that he often had dreams that if he touched her when she died, she would come alive. But when she did die, he did not touch her. 'By that time,' he says, 'I had understood about death, and was afraid that if I touched her she would indeed come alive and that all my waiting and watching would have to be resumed!'

Sri Sri also could not tolerate the pain and suffering that others had to endure. In his house, there was a girl in her teens who would do all the household chores, like cleaning the dishes, washing the clothes, and mopping the floor. While his sister could enjoy herself, this young girl had to do all the menial jobs. They were both of the same age. Such discrimination caused him deep sorrow, and this issue led to his regular quarrelling with the other family members.

Nevertheless, little Ravi Shankar was also a child who loved to play pranks. One day, when his father opened his briefcase in the midst of a meeting in his office, he found it full of toys, instead of his official documents. All his colleagues had a hearty laugh at his expense. In the evening, when he met his son and emptied the briefcase of all the toys, Sri Sri simply laughed and pointed at the piles of his father's papers arranged neatly along with his other toys! Pitaji burst into laughter on seeing his lovely laughing face.

Eager to know more about Sri Sri's childhood, I approached Bhanu, his sister. My first impression of her was that she was beautiful and full of laughter. When I asked her how it felt to be Sri Sri's sister, she just giggled in her characteristic way. She then said: 'I always wanted to be where my brother was. I was not interested in hanging out with my friends. In fact, my parents had to seek special permission so that I could accompany my brother on his class trip!' I then asked: 'Didn't you ever fight with each other?' She replied: 'Whenever I would do something that would displease him, instead of fighting or yelling, he would just go and sit calmly in a corner with his eyes closed. I would go near him and try to get him to speak, but nothing would disturb him. He would just smile!' Sri Sri's paternal aunt recalls: 'Sri Sri would spend a lot of time observing the rituals in churches, mosques, and temples. Whatever he learnt or noticed, he would share it with Bhanu.'

'There was a woman in my life who loved me more than herself,' says Sri Sri. It seems clear that Guruji's mother was the woman who had had the greatest impact on his life. The story of her birth and death is as interesting and as full of mystery as his life. Her parents, while on a pilgrimage to Kashi, considered one of the holiest cities in India, prayed for a child at a temple of the Mother Divine. About ten months later, a child was born. She was named Visalakshi, after the same temple Goddess to whom the parents had prayed. Amma grew up in a simple orthodox South Indian family surrounded by a host of relatives. She had an aunt called Savithri who taught her and her sisters how to sing and play the veena (a large-sized string instrument). As her grasping powers were very good and she could quickly memorize any new ragas taught to her, she mastered these fine arts at a fairly young age. She was also good with languages, and she was very proficient in Sanskrit. She studied in the Government High School for Girls in Papanasam and completed the SSC (Senior School Certificate).

Amma got married to R. S. V. Ratnam in 1955 and moved to Bangalore. She would always be feeding people, and soon the title Annapoorneshwari (Goddess of food) was added to her name. She continued the practice to the very end, and today it is perpetuated by her daughter. Devotees and teachers alike had great respect and affection for Guruji's mother.

This is how Sri Sri reminisces about her today: 'When I was a child, some astrologer told my mother: "Your son was born on Shankar Jayanti day and he is going to leave you. He will become an ascetic." This made her anxious, but I reassured her that I would not leave her. However, all her relatives would berate her: "What has happened to your son?

He talks philosophy, he does not behave like a normal person
.... You better find him a job and get him married quickly."
Then, once again she would feel a little confused for a couple
of days, until Pitaji would console her saying: "Don't worry,
he has very fine stars, he will turn out well, don't worry."
Other people would tell her: "Don't allow your son to do so
much puja [prayer or worship], he may go mad and crazy.
He will not study properly." So every time I would sit for
meditation, she would hurry me up saying: "Not yet over?
You are taking too long. Come on. Study." Sometimes she
would ask me to do sandhyavandana [a ritual supposed to be
performed, three times a day, by those Hindus who wear the
sacred thread] instead of puja. I would go and do it but it would
take me one-and-a-half hours, while my cousins would finish
the same in ten minutes! When I would somehow escape a
sports class, come home and do something else, she would
scold [me]: "Why did you come so early? Go and play football."
But I would look at my feet and think: these feet cannot kick
anybody, let alone the ball, and I would refuse to go.'

Sri Sri recollects how his mother would sometimes hide
all his puja paraphernalia. He would come back from school,
start crying and threaten not to eat till all his things were given
back to him. Even today he states that he acquired all his
degrees only to please his mother and, on her insistence, he
even went for an interview with a bank. But as it turned out,
he interviewed the interviewers instead of the other way
around! They asked him what he was doing. When they
found out that he taught meditation, they got so interested
that they wanted to know more. Sri Sri sat down and gave
a useful discourse on the topic! He was selected and sent a
round-trip ticket to Delhi. However, since he was not interested

in taking up the job, he spent one or two days in Rishikesh (a place of pilgrimage on the banks of the Ganga; now in the state of Uttarakhand) and returned to Bangalore. Knowing that Amma did not want him to go far away from her, he would tease her that he would take up a job in the Merchant Navy, from where he kept getting offers. He comments today: 'Amma didn't wish me to go that far. But she definitely wanted me to take up a job in one of the banks.' When asked if his mother scolded him, Sri Sri smiles and says that she did so when she found him returning from trips with an empty suitcase. He enjoyed sharing all that he had – money, clothes, everything – with others!

Chapter Three

The Celebration That Is Silence

Give me not thirst, if you cannot give me water.
Give me not hunger, if you cannot give me food.
Give me not joy, if you cannot share.
Give me not skills, if I cannot put them to good use.
Give me not intelligence, if I cannot perceive beyond it.
Give me not love, if I cannot serve.
Give me not desires, if they do not lead me to you.
Give me not a path, if it does not take me home.
Give me not prayers, if you will not hear them.

Have you ever witnessed or experienced a religious festival in India? Such festivals are, to say the least, frenzied events. I somehow procured an invitation to attend the Navaratri (literally means 'nine nights') celebrations, which honours the nine aspects of the Mother Divine, at the Bangalore ashram. There it was, and continues to be, a celebration of silence amidst chaos. The atmosphere was simply electrifying. In spite of the huge crowds, there was this incredible energy and serenity that I had never felt before.

After the festivities, we were sitting in a group with Bhanu, when she remarked: 'This is the first Navaratri without Amma.' I suddenly realized it had been one year since she had passed away. Bhanu continued talking about Amma's last days: 'I found her behaviour odd. It was strange that a strong-willed woman like her, who had always been in charge of everything, seemed to be turning over all responsibility. Maybe she was preparing me to take care of the house, children and family. However, she performed all the yagnas [a yagna was a ritual of sacrifice in the ancient times; nowadays, it is a form of worship in which offerings are made to various deities] fully.' The day after Navaratri, she was hospitalized.

When Amma breathed her last in 2000, Sri Sri was at Varanasi. There were about 8000 people whom he had to address the very day he lost the person dearest to him. I was with him that day and saw the depth of his silence, serenity, and patience in attending to everybody in those difficult moments. Yet the smile did not fade. To the devotees who were with Guruji at the time, and knew of his attachment to Amma, it was a lesson in equanimity. Rajshree Patel recalls:'I always knew he loved his mother very dearly, but I did not realize the depth of his love until after she had passed away. At the International Millennium Course in Italy, a month or so after the death of his mother, I discovered yet another dimension to Sri Sri. On the one hand everyone is the same to him, his love is impersonal and yet, I was learning, it was deeply personal. We were sitting in an assembly of 1500 to 2000 people. Someone in the front row was holding a magazine with Amma's photo in it. Sri Sri, with a certain depth in his voice, was speaking of the importance of gratitude in life. After a brief pause he said: "There was a woman in my life who loved me more than herself." Everybody sat up. He gestured to the magazine and added: "She was my mother." A tear of deep love and gratitude for her rolled down his face, and I suddenly felt a total connectedness to him and started crying uncontrollably. And for the first time in all the years that I knew him, I saw the deepest personal love possible, free of attachment and demands, yet full of gratitude.'

Let me now focus on the role played by Guruji's father, R. S. V. Ratnam. When people ask him as to who Guruji is to him, he says: 'My answer is simple: he is both my son and my Master.' Pitaji hails from a prominent family that has been responsible for many path-breaking developmental activities in the state of Karnataka. He is engaged in research on the modern applications of ancient Vedic wisdom. He also has the ability to weave uplifting stories from lifeless words. He basically narrates tales from the Puranas. (The Puranas are a class of literary texts, all written in Sanskrit verse, whose composition dates from the fourth century BC to about AD 1000.) Though in his late seventies, he is a tireless worker for social causes, and guides several projects for the rehabilitation and emancipation of rural women. It is through him that we got to know more about Sri Sri's childhood. He recounts an interesting incident:

In the olden days, big households in rural areas of South India had heavy cradles, in which the child and the mother could swing and sleep. It was also thought to be a status symbol. My wife's ancestors, being the leaders of the village, had built a long single-storeyed house with its front door facing the temple street. The broad corridor-cum-hall of the house had one such big wooden cradle tied to a solid wooden beam above by four heavy iron chains. One day, as I entered the house and approached the cradle, my wife saw me and immediately got up from the cradle to receive me. That was the fatal moment, when, with the child still in it, suddenly all the iron chains holding the cradle snapped and it fell to the ground with a loud noise. When she heard the sound of the crash, the thought of losing the baby was too much for my wife and she fainted. I had to swiftly step forward to hold her in my arms, as I looked simultaneously at the cradle, expecting to see a seriously hurt child under the heavy chains. But, lo [and behold]! Something beyond my comprehension was happening and my head, filled as it was with fear, refused to believe what my eyes were seeing! Was it true or was I dreaming? There, inside the damaged cradle, was the child playfully smiling, while all the heavy chains, instead of falling inside the cradle, had fallen out, defying all laws [of physics]. My sister-in-law, who was nearby, ran to the cradle, picked up the child and cried out in relief: "The boy is safe, the boy is safe." It took some time for my wife to regain consciousness and composure, but when the smiling infant was placed in her arms, she held the baby to her bosom, though a little dazed, and began to laugh and cry at the same time. Later, with trembling hands and tearful eyes, she handed the baby to me, with the words: "God has saved our son."

Pitaji adds: 'When Guruji was around two years old, his mother, while she had work to do, would often make him sit in the corridor of the house facing the garden and point out the birds and other small creatures, which sing and sway with the wind and sun. The young child, with wide-eyed interest, would laugh and clap his hands in glee till he was called back. One day while his mother was preparing his food, she was called out, and before leaving the kitchen, she made him sit at a distance from the stove and said: "Don't go near the stove, the heat will hurt you." When she came back after a while, she found him still sitting calmly, watching with interest the burning stove and boiling water. He had made no attempt to move and looked up at her with his laughing eyes. It was indeed a joy to observe the child's total faith in his mother and her total confidence in him. This totality of faith, confidence, and love blossomed in later years and enveloped everybody around him.'

'Eighteen months after his birth,' continues Pitaji, 'his sister Bhanu came into this world, a fair, restless infant, fond of sweets, toys, and tales – a counterpoint to her brother, who was calm, composed, and confident. I used to say that she was the other side of the coin. When he was shown his younger sister, he bent forward and touched her head and then in childlike innocence asked us: "From where did she come?" For want of a better answer, his mother replied: "The doctor gave her to us." "Will she be taken away?" was his next question. Jokingly I said: "Will you give her away, if the doctor asks you to?" "No," was his emphatic reply, "I will not give her away. She belongs to us." This feeling of protective love for his sister came to the fore often. In fact, respect for elders, love to youngsters, focus on the jobs at hand, and a feeling of belongingness formed the basis of his actions and activities even while he was young. As he grew, these qualities expanded to cover more and more people and today every one of us realizes that he is an apostle of love and confidence.

'Even as a youngster, Gurudev was more concerned about the welfare of others. I recollect the day when my aged mother took him for the first time to the nearby grocer. When they left home, he grasped her hand tightly and she assumed that it was for his security. But she was very surprised and amused when the young fellow cautioned her saying: "Grandma! Be careful. Hold my hand so that you do not fall." His voice had a ring of maturity quite unconnected to his tender age.'

Pitaji also remembers that many saints and seers visited their home. Some of South India's most respected and revered Shankaracharyas (senior pontiffs) – including those of Sringeri (in Karnataka) and Kanchi (or Kanchipuram, in Tamil Nadu) – recognized the divine spark in the young child and blessed him. 'One day, His Holiness Shri Shankaracharya of Shivganga [in Karnataka, near Bangalore] visited our house and accepted [our] puja and offerings. During the celebrations, Amma brought the child out and laid him at his feet. The Acharya saw the lovely face of the baby and noticed some special marks on his back. His eyes shone with joy when he said: "Your child is Divine. You are lucky and blessed to be his parents," and folded his hands in respect to young Sri Sri. Once, we visited a Ganesh temple and the big elephant head of the Divinity fascinated him. "Why does he have such a big head?" he asked, and I replied, "Because he has storage of great knowledge in it." "So people with big heads have more knowledge, is it?" was his next question. I was rather taken aback by this innocent twist in logic, but managed to answer: "It is not quite like that. Ganesh has a big head, but if we pray to him, He will put much knowledge into our small heads too."

'Beggars presented a mystery to my son. "Why are they begging?" he would ask his mother. "Because they are poor," my wife would reply. "But why are they poor?" Being stuck for an answer, she would gently divert him to me. After a vain search for a satisfactory answer, I was forced to say: "God made them poor", since I did not wish to burden the young mind with the harsh karmic theory. But his answer was stunning.

He calmly said: "Then I will ask God, not to make beggars." What a mature resolve from a tender heart!

'When we admitted him into a nursery school next to our home in Bangalore, he became the favourite of both the teacher and the tiny tots. They used to crowd around him and he would tell them the stories he had heard from me. One day, he went to school and was back home shortly, followed by all the boys and girls of his class. To his surprised mother, he calmly said: "The teacher has gone home for some work, and I brought the students home, for some play. Can you please give them something to eat?" On her return to the school the poor teacher was shocked to find the whole class empty. She ran to our house [upon learning that all the children were here] and found them enraptured by his stories. Later when she asked him, why he had taken them all home, he simply replied: "There is so much noise outside, and we all wanted to eat something," forgetting the fact that the children produced more noise inside than what was noticed outside!

'Gurudev was a keen observer and noted all the procedures of puja that the temple priest performed and he would try to emulate them at home. Even when he was only three years old, he had learnt a few mantras. He would often close his eyes and repeat them. When once I asked him what he wanted from the Lord, he promptly said: "I want everyone to be happy. I don't like people quarrelling." Tolerance and joy were the basis of the young Master's attitudes. When Ravi Shankar was four years of age and his sister two, both would chant and pray, much to the amazement of the people around. When asked what it was that they prayed for, pat came the reply: "For everyone to be happy!"'

Chapter Four

The Days with Maharishi

Celebrate while you are alone and celebrate
when you are with people.
Celebrate silence and celebrate noise.
Celebrate life and celebrate death.

In Sri Sri, you find a beautiful blend of Veda and science. The seed (for achieving such a blend) sprouted in him when he came in contact with His Holiness Maharishi Mahesh Yogi, whose Transcendental Meditation (TM) was known the world over. Maharishi was at that time conducting Veda and science conferences all over India and bringing scientists and Vedic scholars together on a single platform. In those days, Dr E. C. George Sudarshan, a renowned professor of physics, former Supreme Court judge, Justice V. R. Krishna Iyer, and the then chief justice of India, Justice P. N. Bhagawati, were travelling with Maharishi. Sri Sri took part in one such meeting in Bangalore. Maharishi Mahesh Yogi spotted the young Ravi Shankar and asked him to accompany him on the tour.

Sri Sri went with Maharishi to Rishikesh and spent some time there. When Maharishi Mahesh Yogi organized a Sant Sammelan (congregation of saints), Sri Sri would be the anchor, welcoming the saints and taking care of their needs. Though Sri Sri was very young, Maharishi recognized his abilities and put him to work. He was thus sent to various places to give talks on the Vedas and science. It was at this time that he started growing a beard, 'to look a little mature', he explains, 'because the people I had to teach meditation to did not take me seriously!' His mother did not necessarily approve of the beard. 'She wanted me to take it off because she was not used to it at all. Here, in the South [almost] everybody is clean-shaven, so it took her a little while to get used to it.'

Very little is known about Guruji's time with Maharishi, but from the few remarks he has made about this phase of his life, it is obvious that it was a momentous period. Maharishi would send Sri Sri to represent him at various matths (monasteries) and ashrams – including the Ordaining Ceremony of Guru Mai Chidvilasanand by her Guru Baba Muktanand. Sri Sri went to Ganeshpuri (Baba Muktanand's ashram located near Bombay) with two truckloads of sweets. Baba Muktanand very warmly received him and the group of pandits accompanying him. Later, Maharishi dispatched Sri Sri to different European countries to give talks on Veda and science. He worked tirelessly to set up Veda, science, and Ayurveda (an ancient system of healthcare native to the Indian subcontinent) centres. In 1980, Maharishi wanted Guruji to organize a big yagna in Noida (a place in Uttar Pradesh, about 20 km away from New Delhi) along with a mammoth Vedic conference. The event turned out to be a big success and Maharishi was so happy that he made plans for an even bigger yagna at Diwali time, which would be performed by 6000 pandits. A few weeks before this event, Sri Sri left with Maharishi for Switzerland and the yagna's preparation was left to others in the organization. Recalls Guruji today: 'Maharishi had his own style of celebrating and did everything with a lot of pomp and show. For this particular ceremony, he wanted everything to be in yellow as far as the eye could see, as this was the colour of Goddess Laxmi. So all the sweets were to be yellow, decorations in yellow, and gold coins from different countries were brought for this yagna ....' But when Sri Sri returned with Maharishi from Switzerland with 3000 Westerners who were to witness the yagna, he realized that there were serious lapses in the arrangements. In fact, many of the pandits who had been recruited were not really what they professed to be. But it was too late. As soon as the puja was over, there was a virtual riot, with all the pandits rushing for the sweets! The foreigners who were there were baffled with what was happening. 'Just to make them comfortable,' recalls Guruji, 'they were told it was a game; it was the tradition!'

Maharishi asked Sri Sri to look into the reasons for the failure of the yagna and the chaos that followed. Sri Sri, through his insight and intuition, quickly found out that kickbacks had been received in the recruitment of the so-called pandits. Since many of them were from the state of Bihar, they spread a rumour that Sri Sri did not like Biharis. Several people cautioned Sri Sri against going to Noida as they anticipated big trouble, but he still went. Waiting for him were around a thousand Biharis with black flags and burning torches who were shouting slogans against him and threatening to set fire to him and his car. He told the leader that they could do what they liked to him, but they should give him half an hour to talk to them. Having secured this reprieve, he told them that he had nothing against Biharis, but that when yagnas were not performed properly, and the chanting of the mantras was not done correctly, it could cause harm to the country and even to the people who perform the yagnas. Then he said that they would be tested and that anybody who was not up to the mark with chanting mantras would be given other work: carpentry, masonry, and so on.

Thus, Guruji in his charismatic manner changed everything around and settled the matter peacefully.

Inevitably, his growing importance in the organization spawned jealousy, and the fact that many worldly men and saints praised Guruji did not help either. Ramnath Goenka, a print media baron and owner of the *Indian Express* group of publications, for instance, who would often meet Maharishi, called Sri Sri 'a beacon of light'. When Maharishi took the young Ravi Shankar to Ananda Mai Ma in Brindavan (a holy place in Uttar Pradesh associated with Lord Krishna), she said to Maharishi: 'Ah, you have brought me the Ganges,' indicating that he was going to purify the world. A famous astrologer of Delhi, Gyanchand Shastri, who had written more than two hundred books, dedicated his book on yoga sutras to Sri Sri. Another time, Guruji met Kotiswamy of Pollachi, in Tamil Nadu, who was reputed to be 400 years old, and asked him for knowledge. Kotiswamy looked at him and said: 'When Shiva himself asks for knowledge, what can I give him?'

Rumours began to spread that Guruji was trying to usurp Maharishi's place. He then thought about leaving, but was reluctant to do so because, at that time, many of Maharishi's aides had deserted him for one reason or the other. Besides, Guruji had a lot of respect for Maharishi, who, he recollects, 'had a lion-like personality, transformed the world, and brought spirituality to the West. He had good energy, was humorous, and was still as a rock when he meditated. He never listened to gossipers and did not like people to complain. If anybody started to complain about someone, he would show them the door.' Maharishi, on his part, was always very proud of Guruji and used to say: 'The sun (Ravi) rises and there will be light everywhere.'

Chapter Five

The Way It All Began

Knowledge is a burden, if it robs you of innocence;
Knowledge is a burden, if it makes you feel you are
special;
Knowledge is a burden, if it gives you an idea that
you are wise;
Knowledge is a burden, if it does not bring you joy;
Knowledge is a burden, if it does not set you free.

In 1980, Maharishi sent Sri Sri to organize another yagna, and asked him to meditate there to ensure the success of the ceremony. Guruji recalls that he used to sit and meditate from 8 a.m. to 4 p.m., with only a half-hour break in between. He would then return in the evenings to attend to Maharishi's lectures, working till 3 a.m. and again be back at the yagna at 8 a.m. He followed this pattern for 40 days. This hectic schedule took a toll on his health, especially as he could not eat properly in Noida and also because of the highly polluted atmosphere there.

As Maharishi wanted to establish Vedic schools all over India, he sent Sri Sri to Bangalore to start the Ved Vigyan Maha Vidya Peeth, but after resting for a while. Pitaji was successful in enrolling 200 children from Karnataka for this school. It was to be an independent set-up as Maharishi did not want to be dependent on government grants and land to start these schools. A trust was formed with Sri Sri, Justice V. R. Krishna Iyer, Lakshman Rao, the mayor of Bangalore, and Justice P. N. Bhagawati. As was often the case, the TM movement soon decided to close down the schools in South India and take all the children to Delhi. This, however, proved to be a disastrous decision, as many of the parents did not agree to the move. Now, the children were left in the lurch.

They could neither return to their old schools as they had spent two years in this new system of education, nor could they go to Delhi, which was not only very far away but also very different from Bangalore as far as language, culture, and food were concerned. This situation may have led to 200 court cases, but Sri Sri personally took on the responsibility to house, feed, and educate all the children.

Most people thought that Sri Sri had gone crazy. How could he possibly shelter and educate so many children without any source of income? But as it happened, just the day the students were to come, some understanding people came forward and offered their houses for the students to stay. Another good Samaritan turned up and offered to look after the arrangements for their food. One after another, miracles happened, and Sri Sri managed the situation effortlessly.

At this juncture, many from the TM movement came down to Bangalore to persuade Sri Sri to stay with the organization. He politely refused. Sri Sri was only a little more than 25 then, but he had already experienced a fair bit of life. He had seen the world from helicopters and bullock carts, travelled to the remotest villages and visited the biggest metropolises. And nothing could sway him. It was during this period, in early 1982, that he decided to observe ten days of silence. Though he was giving talks and lectures, and conducting meditation classes, he felt that something more was needed to make a difference in people's lives. This innate restlessness gave birth to the Art of Living Course and the Sudarshan Kriya. When questioned about these developments, he is reported to have answered that he knew something was 'coming up'.

The first course was held in Shimoga, a city in central Karnataka, near the spectacular Jog Falls. It is said that he remained silent throughout the course. At first the participants were baffled, but slowly they felt he was actually teaching them, communicating knowledge through the sacredness of silence, and when he eventually began to speak, many felt that they had already heard what he had to say. It is also in 1982 that he established the Art of Living Foundation as an educational organization designed to assist all levels of society in achieving their full human potential. For five years Sri Sri taught the courses himself. 'The kriyas used to last from two to three hours, and the courses went on from eight in the morning till eleven at night, with only a small break for lunch at 5 o'clock! I was very tough, in the ego-busting sessions, for instance,' he recalls today.

Of the many stories of Sri Sri's early teachings, I will narrate only a few. Sri Sri was once conducting courses in England. He would meet the public for one hour a day at the house of Poppat-bhai, the owner of a London shoe company. Sri Sri is reported to have healed many people there. For instance, someone who could not walk started walking, someone who could not talk properly began delivering fluent speeches, and Poppat-bhai's daughter, who was suffering from thyroid problems, was healed after only two meditation sessions with Sri Sri. There was also a young boy, Chetan, whose eyes would water constantly because of some rare disease. Sri Sri told his parents that they should tie a pearl with no hole around his neck. But where were they to find this perfect pearl? they wondered. Lo and behold! When they got home, they discovered a pearl without a hole in their altar. They tied it around his neck and he got cured. On another occasion, Sri Sri was staying with the Bharadwaj family, in Southall, London, and he was scheduled to give a talk in a temple. They had just arrived at the temple and only one bhajan had been sung when Sri Sri got up suddenly and said he wanted to go back to the Bharadwaj house. Everyone was surprised but nobody argued with the young Master. Upon reaching the house, they found Mrs Bharadwaj lying on the floor in a state of semi-coma after a severe heart attack. Sri Sri just put his hand on her head and, by the time the ambulance arrived, she was perfectly all right! Upon hearing this news, a large number of people began to queue up, for a desire to be fulfilled, or for getting healed. What seemed clear was that there was very little interest in acquiring knowledge. 'I didn't want people to become greedy, but to blossom in knowledge,' clarifies Sri Sri. To this end, he started the Teachers' Training Course.

Once, while in Assisi, Italy, Sri Sri was taking a walk with a few devotees. He suddenly pointed to a nearby hill and suggested that they walk to the top of it. By the time they got there, it began raining lightly and a pink cloud could be seen on the horizon. On top of the hill was an old chapel. In that chapel was a Catholic priest who did not speak any English. This chapel was not very popular because the priest spoke about reincarnation and wanted to make his church into a multicultural abode. When the priest saw Sri Sri, he was overwhelmed with joy and invited him in. He said that he had a vision that Sri Sri would be visiting and that at that time it would be drizzling and there would be a pink cloud in the sky! The priest revealed how he had never experienced so much love and peace in his whole life as he felt in that one interaction with Guruji. Another time in Italy, again accompanied by a few devotees, Sri Sri suddenly ran towards a bush. Everybody wondered what he was doing. He found a man sitting behind the bush and praying desperately to be 'taken away' by the hand of God. The man was a scuba diver who had had an out-of-body experience while underwater, and had tried many ways to relive it, but without success. When he saw Guruji, he went into in a state of shock and started to follow him wherever he went. Guruji probably gave him what he wanted because one day he disappeared just as mysteriously as he had appeared.

Pitaji's house in Bangalore, from where Sri Sri was conducting most of his work, was really too small for the growing number of projects. Consequently, Sri Sri, with Pitaji's help, started developing an ashram on rocky wasteland on the outskirts of Bangalore.

Pitaji recalls how it all started:

The very first effort to start the Ved Vigyan Maha Vidya Peeth was on 13 November 1981 in Bangalore city. Why 13 November? Because Sri Sri wanted to prove that there is nothing inauspicious about the number 13! We had 150 students who had to be fed, clothed and educated within the small house of Jayanagar [a locality in Bangalore where the Sri Sri Media Centre now stands]. Meanwhile, we were looking for land to establish the ashram: it took us four years to get it sanctioned! In April 1985, we got 60 acres of land leased for 30 years and in October we started on that very spot our very first Sanskrit school with 20 students, and we also quickly transferred the Vedic school there. By October 1985 we had erected temporary buildings, but still had no water. People said that the area was too rocky to find water, but Sri Sri pointed out a certain place and said we should be able to find it there. We started drilling: hundred feet, no water, two hundred feet, three hundred feet, still no water .... The contractor told me it was useless to continue and waste money, but I was sure that if Sri Sri said water was there, it was bound to be. And at 310 feet, water started gushing out!

Within two years we had more temporary buildings made out of brick and red-earth mortar, which housed 20 people, including the cook who stayed in the ashram, but there was still no electricity. At that time, Sri Sri was travelling all over India and the West and did not spend more than one-and-half months per year in the ashram. Thus, for nearly twelve years, I was more or less running the place, though we could all feel his presence, and it was as if he was there all the time, giving us directions. What actually gave us a tremendous boost was the first international conference in 1988 – 80 people attended from all over the world, and it was such a success that, thereafter, it was repeated every two years.

I was also putting a lot of energy into the school – in the beginning, we used to face opposition from other schools, as we were not charging any fees. Added to this was the fact that we asked the children to chant "Vande Mataram" and taught them "Om Namah Shivaya", which made some people say that we were a "communal organization". But soon, not only 100 per cent of our children passed, but also, it was the ...

Christian students who came first in the Bhagavad Gita competition, which showed that actually we were very secular in spirit. Then there was the Vedic Science Research Institute that we set up. In the beginning, the government was very sceptical, but quickly we were able to prove that there are more than 71 scientific disciplines in the Vedas and [then] we were recognized by the government as a serious body.

Rajshree, who was one of my first teachers at the Art of Living centre, adds: 'Sri Sri is so clear in his mind. He is like a mirror. He reflects our true nature. I haven't found anybody with whom I can work with such ease and comfort. At the same time, I cannot cope with his energy. He can go on working for hours without getting tired, and his intentions are very powerful. Simultaneously, he is so childlike.

'While flying from Bombay to Bangalore with him the first time, he said to me: "You will love Bangalore, it is the garden city, and our ashram is so green." I am unable to recall what I was expecting, but the city of gardens had a lot more cement than trees or flowers. The ashram, well, it was barren, dry, hilly, rocky, and infested with snakes. There were three small buildings and huts, which Sri Sri called "temporary housing". Apparently, there had been an international conference in 1988 with about sixty to eighty people. Some of the students at the time were housed there and others … in a nearby facility. The buildings were initially erected for the Vedic pandit boys. Narayana Kutir was a leaky hut with a small room for meditation and [an] even smaller adjoining bedroom for Sri Sri. Shakti Kutir, his current cottage, was just being completed: a small round building with only one room that had a tiny mattress on the floor on one side and a low wooden chair on the other. Until 1994, the cottage was just this, small and simple. Later, two other rooms were added.

'Regardless of the growth of the foundation, Sri Sri and his lifestyle have always remained simple and humble. As the organization grew, more and more people wanted to serve and offer donations. I remember a number of different occasions when either a very wealthy family or an individual would offer to build the entire ashram with all the modern facilities and luxuries. I, who had come from the West, jumped at the idea: no more electricity cuts, no more water shortage, possibilities of having water heaters, airconditioners, etc., but Sri Sri always refused. I never understood why he refused such generous offers till one day he explained to me the idea of Guru Dakshina (the skilful way of giving): "This ashram will bring peace to all those who come here. It is a blessing and a gift to be able to give comfort and peace in life. One can give money, one can give food, but to give peace of mind is the highest gift of all and everyone should partake in that offering. It is as a family that we will build this home."'

Many a time, when we all walked around the ashram, Sri Sri would point to the location of future buildings: 'There will be a coliseum on top of the hill, a kitchen here and the meditation hall there.' He described the land and the location of structures in such detail that I assumed there was a concrete plan laid out on paper. The plan was laid out, only it was not on paper. In response to my question about blueprints, he always smiled and replied: 'In the big blue sky the prints are fixed.' The buildings were constructed, as and when the need for them arose. When the meditation hall was being constructed, at every pillar, within a distance of about 8 feet from each other, different types of soil and minerals were being dug up. Geologically, this phenomenon was inexplicable, but Sri Sri explained that the ancient rishis used the land for yagnas and that was the reason for the variation of soil and minerals within such a short distance.

Our strolls always ended at the top of the hill where the coliseum (Sumeru) stands today. Sri Sri would look out into space and then down the hill, and say: 'One day this whole hill will be covered with thousands of people. There will be an amphitheatre for sitting arrangements, I will not even be able to walk because there will be such a crowd, and there will be a screen where they will have to project everything.' On one level, I knew all that he was saying would happen in the future. On another level, I wondered how everything would be made possible. There were barely eight to ten people coming to the satsang at the time, so the idea of thousands seemed unimaginable. Unknown to all of us, the platform was being laid for the phenomenal growth of the Art of Living in India. Today, when I look back and remember those ashram strolls with Sri Sri, I recall with amazement his quiet yet resolute statement: 'Everything is set.'

Chapter Six

From Student to Teacher

The sun rises and celebrates,
The sky embraces and celebrates,
Winds blow and celebrate,
Rivers flow and celebrate,
Birds sing and celebrate,
Peacocks dance and celebrate,
Trees flower and celebrate,
Buds blossom and celebrate,
We smile and serve,
  meditate and celebrate.

Time passed by but my curiosity never ebbed. By now we had taken many Advanced Courses, and were familiar with many of the Art of Living techniques. But I had seen, during the Advanced Courses, how the TTC (Teachers' Training Course) groups had a special bonding, apart from an incredible abundance of energy and laughter. Such a scenario filled me with a longing to be a part of that joy. Doing the TTC thus seemed a logical progression. We told Guruji we wanted to do this course and he seemed to approve of it – so we went ahead.

I have not spoken so far about the great privilege it is to be born an Indian – and I think this is as good an occasion as any. When I first came to India and met the Mother, I was barely 19 years old. Right from the beginning, I was amazed by the simplicity of the Indian children at the Sri Aurobindo Ashram, in school and at play. What struck me was their capacity to experience joy, their unbounded energy, and their mental and physical elasticity. It made me look at myself and realize how my Western and Christian education had harmed me, making me lose the simplicity, the innocence, and energy I must have had once upon a time. I then used to write to the Mother, telling her of my anguish. She would smile, I was told, upon receiving my letters, and arrange flowers for me on a plate. She would say that each flower had a particular vibration and aim: 'aspiration, simplicity, endurance, Divine grace.' Today, having spent so many years in India, I have touched upon, to some degree, the source of this joy and simplicity. Whenever I address Indian audiences, I tell them that it is a great privilege to be born an Indian, as they naturally inherit qualities that have been practised for millennia by their forefathers and which are, so to say, imbedded in their genes: tolerance, gentleness, devotion, and the ability to overcome difficulties. I found that many of these qualities manifested themselves in our fellow participants of the TTC.

As for my wife and I, at the start, we were still quite confused about whether or not we really wanted to become teachers. 'Blessed are those who are confused,' affirms Guruji, but it is not an easy state of mind. We were disciples of Sri Aurobindo and the Mother, lived in Auroville, and there was no question of ever going back on those realities. 'Feel at home everywhere,' Guruji often told us, probably sensing our torment. He would never pressurize us, never ask us to bow to him, and never ask us when we were returning next to the ashram. Yet, we were still torn by our inner conflict, of 'betraying' Sri Aurobindo and the Mother, not understanding that God is one. Nonetheless, Namrita and I finally completed our TTC and became teachers seven years after we were first introduced to the Art of Living. It was one of the most momentous phases of our lives.

People ask us: What is it like to be an Art of Living teacher? How does it feel? What do you have to do? I can only speak for myself. It is an awesome responsibility and, above all, a great honour. I have had a fairly successful career as a journalist and writer. I have interviewed five Indian prime ministers, met many high-profile personalities, had books published, addressed packed audiences, but nothing makes me prouder than being an Art of Living teacher. It is fine to do well in worldly life, but how can you beat sharing with others a special knowledge that not only helps you to become a better person, but also directs you towards unknown realms of joy and sweetness, and helps you to discover an untapped source of energy in your Self?

Unlike in most other organizations, the Art of Living teachers represent every background, religion, and nationality one can think of. It is like a bouquet of assorted flowers, or as we sometimes jokingly say, 'a box of assorted nuts': the serene Bharat; the loud and bubbly Vikram; the gentle and shy Anurag; the strong and commanding Vinod; and the blonde and delicate Nathalie! So diverse are the people and their tendencies, yet they all feel at home with Sri Sri, which is a phenomenon in itself. I marvel at his patience in dealing with them all.

I sometimes wondered how Guruji would select anyone and everyone as a teacher. I used to feel that teachers should have basic qualifications or, at the very least, a certain talent. I was proved wrong. I would say now that a good teacher is one who is committed, has integrity, compassion, and an unwavering attitude towards service. Of course, all teachers are not the same: there are those who live the knowledge wholeheartedly and others who deliver the knowledge very well but live it only partially. But I came to understand that it is not the talent that really matters. Many lecturers and professors give scholarly discourses, but they don't make an impact on one's life; but here, a teacher delivers the simple truths of life and brings about a definite transformation.

Guruji once said in a teachers' meeting: 'Do not use knowledge for your mistakes, but as an umbrella.' When asked by someone why he keeps training new teachers when some of them may not be of a very high calibre, he answered: 'You can never judge anyone because you do not know what diamond is present where .... Truly, the world is diverse: some people may grow by teaching, and each one can guide everybody else to whatever extent they can.' In conclusion, being an Art of Living teacher is like carrying an invisible badge on your chest, which makes you feel: 'I carry an invaluable knowledge. I help in bringing happiness and harmony to humanity. I am the flag bearer of a new world order. Blessed am I to have been chosen amongst so many.'

And it is teachers who form the backbone of the Art of Living movement, and it is through them that Guruji reaches out to so many people. They are his ambassadors, the carriers of his message, and the instruments of his force.

Kishore saw Guruji for the first time in 1985 during a Basic Course. He was impressed by a brochure that declared: 'Come and meet your Self.' Thinking that Ravi Shankar, the world-renowned sitarist, was conducting the course, he found another Ravi Shankar (Sri Sri) himself teaching what is now known as the Art of Living Basic Course. The introductory 40-minute meditation was so powerful that he completely lost track of time. He was working as an engineer then, travelling all over the world, but he soon started organizing Basic Courses. A couple of years later, Kishore attended an informal Teachers' Training Course – the first one ever – which was conducted by Guruji himself. The notes taken by the participants formed the *TTC Manual*. Kishore then started teaching – only two people to begin with, but slowly his flock kept growing. He shifted permanently to the ashram in 1991, which he says was an exhilarating but demanding phase of his life. He, along with the other people there, did a lot of physical work: from digging holes for planting trees to carrying pipes. When I asked him what he considers to be the biggest miracle Guruji ever performed, he replied: 'Love is the biggest miracle! How tears turn into smiles in seconds by being with him, how unfriendly people turn out to be compassionate!' Kishore fondly remembers how once, while travelling along with Guruji in a plane, a particularly rude lady turned friendly and warm after just one glance from Guruji.

It was seva time and I was watering the plants. As I watched those fragrant jasmine flowers, it occurred to me how they grow on their own – all that we can do is water them a little bit! The same is true in our life. I realized that with knowledge as the water that nourishes, life starts bearing flowers like this jasmine plant. I saw Sharmila, who teaches the Art Excel and Young Adult Courses, playing hide and seek with kids. It brought to mind what Guruji often tells parents: 'Your concern is how soon your kids will grow up. My concern is when you will become kids again!' When I first heard this statement, it sounded ridiculous, but now I know how much sense it makes. The way Sharmila could harness youth energy here was impressive. The teenagers seemed to have overcome inhibitions; they were communicating freely with people of all age groups. I asked Sharmila about her journey with Sri Sri.

'There is so much I want to say about my Guru – the feelings are so profound, the words so inadequate. We have received so much from him – so much love, grace, knowledge, joy, the nectar of life. Life has been transformed so miraculously. Every moment is so breathtakingly beautiful that the only wish seems to be to share everything. Life is gorgeous, life is fun and I am in eternal gratitude to my Guru who straightened me out, brought me out from my web of fear and insecurities, and opened in me a fountain of love, joy, and enthusiasm. He has made me aware of the sheer magnificence of our lives, of the human body, of our very existence. Events [sometimes calamitous] continue to happen, but now they do not shake me.'

A little later, I came upon a giggling gang of Art of Living teachers and decided to take them all out for a pizza, hoping to get more insights into Sri Sri's life. At the restaurant, one by one, they started telling their stories and were so enthusiastic about their narration that sometimes they would all speak together! I was impressed by the diversity of the 'assorted nuts' and their unique experiences with Sri Sri.

Urmila Agarwal, an Indian who had lived in Germany for many years, was tired of her 'spiritual shopping' when some Swiss friends invited her to meet an Indian yogi visiting Berne in 1988. This is what she had to say: 'My Guru has a name, yet he is formless, eternal beyond time and space. He is much more than this. I know him and yet I do not know him. What I do know is that he has given a meaning and direction to my life and brought fulfilment to it. In his presence, I experience the Almighty who dwells in every heart. His merest touch sweeps away the karma of lifetimes, burns away ignorance, and brings divinity to shine through human beings.

'I used to think that the guru–disciple connection was also a type of relationship. With Guruji I have experienced that it is beyond all relationships. It is multicoloured and multidimensional, because it is the relationship to one's own reality, the Truth. He is everything for me – he is my parent and my child, my brother, my sister, and my friend. He has cooked and served me when I was tired and hungry. He has given me whatever I needed, before I even asked for it. He has taken my pain away before it would turn into suffering. He has made me immortal before I die. He has always talked to me in the silent moments – now I can hear him.

'In August 1988 when my friends invited me to meet an Indian yogi, I was searching for a Guru, someone who would take me into the mysteries of the unknown. It was a point in my life when I had almost given up the search because I could not find satisfaction anywhere and once again doubts popped up in my mind. So, after a second thought, I picked up the phone and called my friends and wanted to have a word with the yogi. He answered my questions, his voice very soothing, and in a few minutes my doubts were replaced by a strong feeling of belongingness and joy. Now I wanted to see him in person, so we drove to Berne. When we arrived there I was a little surprised by the young and delicate looking person clad in white, with a radiant face and an unusually simple personality. For the first time I felt that this was the pivotal day of my life. Still thinking myself very smart, I interviewed him and after spending some hours with him, half-heartedly I left for Basel. But there was something I was very happy about – he asked me to come to Bangalore for the International Advanced Course in the month of December. This meeting was very special and powerful, a deep experience of joy and celebration. In fact it was the most precious day of my life.'

Arun Madhavan was the area director with the Standard Chartered Bank in Bombay, who was looking for 'breathing space' amidst his hectic work pattern and lifestyle, when he came across the Art of Living Course. The immense benefits from the workshop he attended made him sit up and take notice of all its benefits; he has since grown to be a teacher and a singer. Arun recalls: 'I met my Gurudev in the mid-1980s, interestingly, in circumstances linked to breath and music. The place of my work, then, was a prestigious bustling business district, in the vortex of heavy traffic and the attendant pollution. I was looking for freedom to breathe! The Healing Breath Workshop that Guruji conducted gave me that freedom and much, much more. It opened up my hidden passion to sing bhajans and experience the ecstasy of Nadabrahma [can be loosely translated as 'the world of divine sound']. In the years that followed, I began to discover the many facets of the Guru, but even after so much time, I realize only the tip of the iceberg has been seen. While discussing the agenda for teachers, he always gets them to think of the "seva" aspect in life. Nothing can sum it up better than the spontaneous words he uttered: "In the Art of Living, we care for the world, we care for you." I have noticed his approach of helping very ordinary people to blossom into radiant individuals. Whenever anyone begins to take a tough stand, he entreats him to see the other viewpoint. He does make people working with him cope with the extreme dualities of simplicity and complexity. The remarkable feature of his presence can be seen in the zeal with which children, teenagers, youth, and seasoned elders flock around him. He has something to offer everyone. There is always humour flowing through his conversations.

'Once a devotee, rather embarrassed to talk about his occupation, said: "Guruji, I am in the liquor business, but I intend to stop it." Guruji replied: "Oh! You are in the business of intoxicating people. So am I, but I don't intend to stop it!"

I have seen his grace flowing in full measure to all those who work with a selfless agenda. Without any doubt, such a soul rarely walks our planet. We are indeed blessed.'

Michael Fischman, our own Basic Course teacher, was also in the group. Michael remembers how surprised he was when he first came to the ashram in 1991. 'There were no trees, no buildings, just a few kutirs, and a thatch roof hall,' he recalls. 'We were preparing for an Advanced Course that was to happen that summer. I was a doubter. I couldn't understand how 200 people could come to the ashram and stay. Gurudev said that it would all just happen. At the time, we just had enough roof space to accommodate around 40 people. Yet somehow, when the time came, 200 people were accommodated easily! It was the most amazing thing, a magical experience. There was enough food for everybody. There were enough beds for everybody and there were no complaints! When I returned years later, it was like coming to an oasis. The transformation was mind-boggling. How did all this manifest from land that was just rock? It can only be the grace of the Guru. Over the years of teaching thousands of people, I have been witness to so many experiences of participants. Some Christians have the experience of Christ during their Sudarshan Kriya, while recently, in the Middle East, people experienced the "Koran reading" happening during the Kriya.'

John Osborne, the bubbly guitarist entertaining our group, was a successful stock broker in the US when he met young Sri Sri for a few moments. In those moments, he intuitively felt that he had come back to his teacher, and attended the Art of Living Course with his wife that weekend at Santa Barbara. 'I remember so clearly the day I met Gurudev,' he told us. 'Within the first five minutes of being in his presence,

I experienced an explosion of pure joy. In just five minutes, I felt closer to Gurudev than I had to my earlier spiritual teacher in fifteen years. Huge waves of gratitude and relief swept over me! As a child, I had felt the protective presence of Christ. As I grew older, that presence had faded. I thought I had lost it forever, but the moment I saw Gurudev, that vibration immediately made its presence felt. Somehow I knew that I had been graced to meet someone who has attained the highest consciousness possible in the human form. My wife and I took the Basic Course in Santa Barbara that weekend, and another in Los Angeles the next weekend, and then another in San Francisco the next! The courses were so lively! A week later, we found ourselves in silence on an Advanced Course in Quebec.'

Gurudev is fond of changing roles right in front of our eyes; playing a mischievous trickster one moment, then appearing in the evening as a Divine Mother, cooking dinner for all of us and, still later, becoming stern, strong, and dispassionate in the face of a misbehaving devotee. He has total knowledge of his devotees that can either be comforting or startling. From my first days with him, he told me things about my past that I had never shared with anyone, and he often appeared to know me better than I knew myself. He somehow keeps individual track of all the hundreds of thousands who consider themselves his devotees. Often he will say, 'so-and-so is thinking of me now', or 'so-and-so is going through a hard time', or 'so-and-so is in pain', even though that person may be thousands of miles away. His presence goes beyond his physical form.

Hailing from the royal family of Thrissur (in Kerala), our good friend Raghu Raj Raja was an ardent communist as a student. After doing Art of Living Courses, he found the common roots of 'caring and sharing' between communism and spirituality. 'I first heard about The Art of Living in 1992 from my friend Narayanan, and attended an introductory talk by Dr Eberhardt, an Art of Living teacher from Germany. Though very impressed at that time, I promptly forgot all about it. A few months later, I heard that there was a TV interview with Sri Sri Ravi Shankar. Something stirred within me, but I had to attend a meeting of a student body closely associated with the Communist Party in Kerala. There were about a score of us in the meeting. As the time for the TV interview drew near, I lost interest in the proceedings and started thinking of a way to sneak out. I was initially hesitant, worried that my absence would be noticed, but I decided that I would go to watch the interview; I did, and I liked what I saw, yet, with my busy schedule, once again I put him out of my mind. The next year in January, I chanced upon a small news item that Sri Sri Ravi Shankar would be in Thrissur, at a place very close to my house. I rushed to the venue and found that he would be there at 7 p.m. for a satsang. I did not know what a satsang was, yet I was there at the appointed time. Sri Sri came, sat, spoke a few sentences, but he was quite unlike my idea of a guru for he had none of the expected high-handed behaviour. He was very simple, very natural, as though he was one of us. It was love at first sight! He then sang Shivoham and we all sang along with him. I really loved it – the words, and the tune stayed on with me long after Gurudev had left. Many people went up to meet him, but I felt shy and stayed in my seat, even though I was drawn to him. The whole of the next day was spent just waiting for 7 p.m. to arrive. I even excused myself from a family outing so that I could be there at the satsang. Gurudev floated in by 7.05 p.m. His talk was inspiring – I was soon to realize that his talks are never anything else. After the satsang, once again people queued up to take his blessings but I stood where I was, gazing lovingly at him. As Gurudev passed by, he smiled at me.

'My first event at the ashram was the Rudrabhishek puja. I initially wondered why he had to perform such a ceremony. This was the twentieth century, wasn't it? Still I attended and was totally entranced by the light and beautiful manner in which he conducted it. It was a unique and beautiful experience, quite unlike pujas that I had experienced elsewhere. By now, deep within my heart, I knew that all I wanted was just to be with him but I didn't say anything. I went to the ashram for Navaratri that year with a big suitcase. At the end of that week, Gurudev said I could stay on at the ashram! He said: "This is your home. Be here, be happy. Celebrate." This was when the growth really started happening in me. He put me through so many different situations. I failed here and there, but slowly I became stronger and more aware.'

A gemmologist by profession, Sangeeta Jani was designing fashion jewellery in Bombay after having studied in the United States. Looking for life beyond humdrum existence, Sangeeta attended the Art of Living Course. As she progressed through the Advanced Course, being of service appealed to her, and she took to teaching the Divya Samaj Nirman (Creating a Divine Society) Courses to encourage volunteerism and the spirit of service. 'Obviously there is no knowing the guru,' she told us in her high-society Bombay accent. 'The only way I know him is through the way I feel and the experiences I have had around him. But each time I thought that I came a little close to knowing him, he would show me a new aspect and confuse me. My first encounter with him was an experience in itself. In December 1992, one evening as I stood in front of the mirror, painting my face for another routine evening out, I thought to myself: "How can I follow a herd of people who make a lifestyle out of working, partying, and shopping? This is definitely not why we were created. There has to be another reason." I looked around and prayed: "I know you are here. I know that you are aware of all my actions and thoughts and you know me better than I know myself because you created me. I am asking you for guidance. Show me the path and the reason for my being here. Please let me be a vehicle for your will, who or whatever you are. Please talk to me."

'A few days later, an acquaintance asked me if I wanted to do a course called the Art of Living. Taking this as a divine message, I did attend, and I loved it! Next I wanted to go to Rishikesh for the Advanced Course. As anticipated, my parents refused to let me go to a strange place all alone, so I gave in. But the next morning a strange phenomenon occurred. Totally unexpectedly, my father himself asked me to go and have a good time. There was a bomb scare at the Delhi airport the day I arrived. Unfazed, my only thought was to meet him. He was sitting in a car. He turned around, looked at me and said: "So! You are here." He was expecting me! I felt all the tension leave my body and sensed that I was being drawn into a kind of love that I had been looking for. I knew instantly that my life would never be the same again. I was here to serve.

'My birthday was approaching. "What's the big deal?" I thought. Another year, another birthday. It would have been nice if I had a boyfriend. I would have had a nice romantic evening. Surprisingly, I got permission to arrange a satsang at home on my birthday, when Guruji would be in town! I finally had something to do. Yet, strangely, I felt a tinge of regret that I would not be able to have a night out with my friends. The day finally arrived and Gurudev walked in! He did more than any human being could do to make it the most interesting birthday I had ever had. We had a great satsang. All my friends who were allergic to the word guru, sat there with tears of love and joy in their eyes. They had experienced deep love. That is when I realized that when you have a guru, the extent of his love is unfathomable. There could be thousands of people around him, but he is constantly aware of each one of them. He ensures all our desires are fulfilled even before we realize them.'

The 'naughty' boy of our group, Naushad, who hails from an affluent Muslim family in Bombay, found the Art of Living Course to be a wonderful therapy. 'I used to suffer from kidney stone attacks, which were frequent and painful. A few days before I was to have an operation, I took the plunge and did the Advanced Course. After completing the course and practising the Sudarshan Kriya for about three weeks, I went for my pre-operative check-up, where it was diagnosed that the stone had disappeared.' Amazed by this phenomenon, Naushad did the Teachers' Training Course, and he now does what he likes doing best – teaching the Art of Living course in Pakistan.

Vinod Kumar was born and raised in Kuwait where he led a rather boisterous life until he chanced on Guruji at a Bangalore Management Association meeting. Vinod has had some of the most incredible experiences with Guruji. 'What I love about my relationship with Gurudev,' he told us in his booming voice, 'is how he creates an event for everything that he wants to teach us. He told me once that Krishna had said to Arjuna: "Whatever is charming in the world, I am the charm. I am the attraction itself, behind the event." Once I attended a fashion show at Delhi, and later went to the venue where Gurudev was staying. At about 8.00 p.m., Gurudev gave darshan. Outside his room there was a raised pathway about two feet high, with a lawn on either side. There were about a hundred people waiting on each side when Gurudev came walking out onto the pathway. It was an astonishing sight. Never in my life had I seen anything like it. It was nothing less than God coming down to earth. Such majesty, beauty, radiance and those flowing robes ... it was a sight to behold, the way he carried himself that day. Then he looked at me and winked mischievously. No words were spoken but since then, I have never felt the desire to go to a fashion show.

'One day in 1992, we were driving with Gurudev from Tezpur [in Assam] airport to Itanagar in Arunachal Pradesh. Along the way, we stopped for a while and Gurudev suggested that we both go for a walk. About five minutes into the walk, Gurudev said: "Let's go into one of those houses." I assumed he wanted to rest so I pointed to one of the better houses on the road. Gurudev said: "No, maybe another house," and we kept walking. After a few minutes, I spotted another inviting house which had several airconditioners mounted in the windows. I said: "Gurudev, this seems to be a convenient place to rest. Let's go into this one." He replied: "Let's keep walking." After a few more minutes, he pointed towards a shabby ill-kept dwelling and said: "Why not go into that house?" Despite my protests, he started walking towards the house and I followed him to the gate. On the right-hand side was a big hut. Looking inside, we saw pictures of all the local gurus and deities. As we walked towards the main house, a lady came out and greeted us. We exchanged pleasantries. As we were leaving, Gurudev turned to me and asked "How much money do you have in your pocket? Give all of it to this lady." I was surprised at the request but I fished 780 rupees out of my pocket. As I was giving it to her, her son came running from the back of the house crying: "Mother, I did not get the 750 rupees I went to borrow." "Don't worry son, we have the money now!" the mother gratefully replied. It turned out that the boy's father was in the hospital and they desperately needed the money for medical expenses. That day I learned a valuable lesson: this is how God comes in many different ways to a devotee, in time of need.'

The only one who had kept silent during this boisterous evening was Prashant Rajore, a chemical engineer from the Indian Institute of Technology, Bombay. Prashant was cured of both his asthma and shyness after the Art of Living Course. 'Before coming to the Art of Living I was a very angry person, and at the same time very shy,' he confessed. 'I had few friends and would hardly talk to anyone, as I lacked self-confidence. On top of that, I was suffering from asthma. One fine day, Bawa (a fellow student from the IIT and a future teacher) just said: "Come and do this course. You will learn some breathing technique which might help you with your asthma." For two months I could not do it, because I could not arrange the course fees, but it was always at the back of my mind. Finally, as I went home one weekend, somebody gave me a sum of money. I don't know who it was, but I just put it in my pocket and as I sat in the train, I felt the money and I thought: "That takes care of the Basic Course and I can spend some on travelling and food, etc. I don't have to worry about anything now!"

'The next day, I went for the course which was outside the IIT campus [in Powai, a suburb of Bombay]. I was very, very stiff and felt extremely shy. I started looking for Bawa, but he was not there; then I saw Dong (the nickname of Harish Ramachandran) – at last a familiar face! So I went up to him, and stuck with him. During the first Sudarshan Kriya, I suddenly smelt some very beautiful fragrance and I thought the teacher might have lit some agarbatti [incense stick]. Then I started feeling dizzy and lost awareness, which made me believe that they were using agarbatti for putting us in an unconscious state. When I woke up, people were already talking about their experience, but I kept quiet and did not share anything. Then I had some problems and Bawa, who had become a teacher, took me in his course. After the first Kriya Bawa said I was almost dancing. After the second session, suddenly when I looked to one side I saw Guruji walking in and thought: "Oh … this is the person I have wanted to meet for a long, long time." I had always had this feeling that some guru was going to come into my life and I would have to go with him. There is a temple opposite my house, where Shankaracharyas and other gurus used to come. My father was a trustee so he would take me in just to look at them, but I had never felt a resonance with any one of them. However, the moment I saw Guruji the first time, I knew this was the person. And then he came and just sat in the course. But then I noticed him gazing at me persistently, and became more and more stiff and self-conscious. When it was over, I heaved a sigh of relief. But Bawa took me to the house where Guruji was staying and I found myself practically alone with him. Again he started looking at me and I got more and more embarrassed, but he kept smiling at me.

'There was an evening satsang near that house, and I found myself enthusiastically singing bhajans. Then Guruji said: "Does anyone have any questions?" As people started asking him questions, I still felt shy and remained silent though there were two questions that had bothered me for years. Then he started talking and suddenly I realized, hey! this is the answer to my first question ... after a while he looked at me and said: "Samjhe (understood)?" But I thought it was just a coincidence, and only if he answered my second question would I believe that something special had happened. Sure enough, soon I realized that he was talking about my second question! Again he said: "Understood?" and looked at me. I thought, this person is very dangerous, and now I can't run away from him! After satsang, I just went and touched his feet as he was leaving.'

Rajshree was also with us that night. 'I have carefully observed, judged, doubted, disagreed, and even fought with Sri Sri', she divulged. 'After all, having been a lawyer, that too, a prosecutor for the Los Angeles District Attorney's office and the United States Attorney's office, judging and analysing came easily and naturally. It has never been easy for people to recognize the Divine. During the life of Krishna only three knew of his essence, only twelve recognized the Christ, and a few recognized the Buddha. I am sure the biggest quandary of the enlightened is revealing the ultimate truth.

'I have been travelling around the world for twelve years, teaching and spreading the knowledge, wisdom, and techniques of Sri Sri Ravi Shankar. In my travels, I have met many sceptics who decide at first glance that "this is not possible". There is an immediate judgement. People have a need to find an inherent weakness either in the teacher or the technique. It is the nature of the mind to hang on to negativity. My response has always been the same. To smile and to know that doubt is always about positivism. This is one lesson I have learnt from Sri Sri. We doubt in the honesty of people, not in their dishonesty. We doubt our capabilities and not in our weakness or incapability. Somehow people associate spirituality, guru, and service with being irrational and illogical. True science and true logic require personal experience. A fair exposure to the Art of Living Courses [and] a few days spent in silence looking at one's self [are] enough to truly come to a reasonable conclusion. I have personally taught thousands of people around the world, from all religions and backgrounds and I have yet to meet a person who didn't benefit beyond words. Prophets come and go, but the egoistic person waits for the future and glorifies the past. By hanging on to the Christ and the Buddha of the past we create division and conflict. Sri Sri and the Art of Living are about the present, unity and harmony. It is about the simple truth that behind every desire is the search for joy, the search to appreciate life. Eating, sleeping, procreating, and collecting things [are] merely existing; appreciating every moment fully is the art of living.'

It was well into the night, and the pizzeria joint was shutting shop. As the rather unique 'family get-together' drew to an end, I felt as though I had lived the lives of these many teachers, fired by an inspiration called Sri Sri. A guru with a mission: to make life a celebration.

Chapter Seven

The Frame That Holds the Picture

Enlightenment is the journey from the head back to the heart, from words back to silence, getting back to our innocence in spite of our intelligence. Knowledge should lead you to that beautiful point of 'I don't know'.

Yogis, saints, and seers are a great mystery to the human mind. How can one understand them? How can we analyse them with our limited intellectual capabilities? And then, how does one define the Divine? And put Him on paper? Our small mind is quite incapable of comprehending the vastness, intricacy, and immensity of love that is behind each of His human incarnations – and it perpetually doubts, particularly when in the presence of the Divine. How many recognized Christ for what he was in his lifetime? How many recognized the Buddha? Doubt has always been the principal impediment to spiritual progress and this holds particularly true when we are in the presence of gurus, as we have a tendency to either question their divinity or our own perceptions of them. Each Master is an expression of Infinity as is our consciousness. But we like to label ourselves and so also our Masters.

Sri Sri is 'label-less'; he is a guru to one, a friend to another, serious one moment, mischievous the next. You cannot contain him in a book. Being with him, all the labels start to drop off and freedom dawns. In his words: 'Only when we are free, can we bring freedom to others.' He sets the example in many different ways. Namrita and I, of course, have had our share of doubts regarding Guruji, and even now there are times when I cannot fathom some aspect or the other of his.

Yet, our itinerary is interesting because it is one of 'doubting witnesses', who slowly, with their own eyes, have observed one or the other facet of him, which makes him so special. Here, I shall make a few attempts at putting down fleeting impressions of Guruji, both mystical and worldly. Of course, they are mine and I hope I will be forgiven if, at times, I appear to err, or even be slightly irreverent.

Sri Sri the Mystic

Whoever wants to witness the divinity behind Sri Sri has just to watch him meditate: nobody can cheat at that game! I remember a very old and wise swami, who, seeing Guruji slip so easily into meditation, tried to imitate him, but he could not do it, however much he tried. After some time, he would always start fidgeting, moving his hands, opening his eyes .... Guruji can stay immobile for hours and you can actually see him recede inwards – his eyes reaching upwards, his hands and body becoming very still, his consciousness slowly reaching planes which are not accessible to us. The mystical air that surrounds Guruji during puja and at satsangs is natural and unpretentious. The whole environment becomes so homely and comfortable, that you become like a child. Sometimes in satsangs his body goes into different postures or mudras. In those moments the atmosphere becomes charged, though it is not an everyday phenomenon. It certainly happens on Navaratri – the festival days of Mother Divine – and on Shivratri, when people gather from all over the world at the ashram. It is an intense, electrifying experience. I have watched him in public satsangs attended by thousands of people, greeting every one with the same smile, showing no sign of weariness. Every

Monday, he does the Rudra Puja himself. When asked why does he perform the puja himself if he is Divine, his reply was simple: 'Puja is a play of the Divine with itself.'

On a particular day in October/November (during the Dusshera festival), Hindus worship vehicles, instruments, tools, and anything they can lay their hands on, including a simple screwdriver. Their belief is that the divine dwells in every atom, a true understanding of the all-pervasiveness of divinity. Such a belief may sound ridiculous from a Western point of view, yet its depth has its own beauty. The Vedic chanting by young boys, the melodious music emanating from women in colourful attire, the beating of drums, and the playing of musical instruments, all add to the magic of the festival. I have always been amazed by the richness and spiritual wealth of India. Sri Sri goes into silence for a few days at this time. Yajnas (Vedic rituals) for peace and harmony are performed at the ashram. On the last day, as the atmosphere has been thus so incredibly charged with energy, devotion, and a sense of timelessness, the kalash (urn) of water, which seems to have a life of its own, is ceremoniously carried around the pandal (a kind of large marquee) with Guruji in front. People join their hands in prayer, some even cry; one cannot miss the flow of grace at these times. There seems to be a common belief that people's desires are fulfilled on this occasion, though I have not heard it from Sri Sri himself.

Raghu, who has spent a long time with Guruji, vouches for his equanimity. He has never found Guruji affected or ruffled by anything in his long association with him. I have myself noticed how people rush to garland him, put a crown on his head, dive to touch his feet, pull his cheek, or touch him. The constant attempt by the disciples at grabbing the

Master's attention and love, this competition for one look from him, one smile, a few words, are taxing. But in spite of all the chaos around him, Sri Sri retains a very profound and deep silence, an unfaltering smile that never loses its serenity. I often wonder how this short-statured man can handle all that day after day! And he treats everybody equally, from the lowliest to the prime minister, from the senior teacher to the new seeker. A child-like glee can be seen on his face, while opening a gift pack or meeting someone new.

It is an unforgettable sight to watch Sri Sri walk through a darshan line. It is as if a cloud of love is floating around him. For many it is a dream come true; for some others it is a moment of confusion where all their traditional concepts of gurus are shattered. Sri Sri is not a very demonstrative person. Yet there is no doubting the immense love he constantly exudes to everyone around him and to the world in general. You start noticing it gradually: in case you are feeling low or depressed, he passes by and he just looks at you once and immediately you become aware that you have lightened up, and that you have found joy and peace within you. Sometimes, for no reason at all you feel like crying in his presence: these are not tears of sentimentality or sadness, but expressions of the inner being suddenly awakening in you and seizing your external emotional self. That Sri Sri is a people's person has been evident right from his schooldays. His sister Bhanu recalls instances of students from senior classes in his school coming to him for counselling and guidance not only in the personal sphere but also in academic areas.

How does one discern or appreciate the love of Sri Sri – and fall in love with him? By watching him – performing meditation, attaining samadhi (a state of intense concentration), interacting with his disciples, noticing his untiring attention towards everybody, observing his boundless patience with his devotees, and realizing his selfless dedication to every aspect of life that needs to be addressed. Usually, a relationship with a great, loving, enlightened, and selfless guru does not fail us like a human relationship: gurus never demand anything from us and are constantly giving. In fact, there are five aspects that blossom in you when you come in contact with a genuine guru: joys well up, shortages disappear, sorrow vanishes, faith grows, and knowledge becomes purposeful. But for all this to happen, your devotion to the guru has to be spontaneous, free, childlike, and ego-less. And how devotees love their Sri Sri: they don't fall in love, but rise instead.

The Human Master

Guruji possesses unsurpassed human qualities. He has, for instance, a phenomenal memory: he never forgets a name, although he says he occasionally does so! The man must have millions of devotees today, but he remembers a face seen two years ago and will always have a kind word of welcome for you, asking about your comfort and inquiring about what you are doing. Guruji speaks several languages, yet is never shy to ask for a word that he does not know, or to verify with an American disciple the exact pronunciation of a slang expression he has just discovered. He utters words with relish, as they are meant to convey states of mind. So you have to be very careful when you listen to him, because every word has its own significance.

Does he think like we do? That is the great mystery. As a yogi he must have a silent and quiet mind, yet he also has an incisive, practical intellect of immense capacity: I have seen him plan out several events and actions in precise detail, though, at the same time, he has demonstrated a grasp over the overall picture. The energy that he expends would leave a normal human being drained and exhausted. He is actually a thinking guru. He chooses his teachers according to his needs. If he needs a teacher in Honolulu, for instance, he will select one, regardless of his or her apparent qualities. Or else, he will earmark teachers who can be useful in particular fields. Even though he seems to act at random and even though the person chosen does not appear particularly worthy or fit spiritually, not only does he or she become a good teacher, thanks to the force that Sri Sri puts behind him or her, but also probably, he or she was destined to be chosen in spite of all factors to the contrary. This is the secret of Sri Sri. I count myself amongst those who fit into that category and so will quite a few teachers reading this book. He is like a switchboard to which anybody can connect himself or herself. 'It is not necessary that the switchboard knows who is connected,' he once pointed out. And it is true: whoever thinks of Guruji often feels that he responds in some way – questions get answered and problems get solved. Whoever is distressed or in difficulty often receives help by praying silently. The role of the switchboard is to be the go-between; this is exactly what Guruji does, like all gurus, by acting as the intermediary between you and the Divine. He is also extremely intuitive. He can fathom the content of a book by reading a few lines; he can know at a glance exactly what state of consciousness you are in; or he can assess a situation by sensing its diverse aspects in a few seconds.

The immense sacrifice that all gurus and saints make, when they are manifest upon this earth, becomes evident from the fact that, while retaining their divinity, they take on some of the earth's pain and agony. They become human and they accept the rules of humanity, which is subject to suffering, illness, and death. There is actually no need for gurus and saints to be physically nailed to the cross: they are crucified every moment by their disciples, who keep throwing their doubts and petty thoughts at the Master. It is said that the South Indian sage, Ramana Maharishi (1879–1950), died of cancer, because he had voluntarily swallowed all the impurities of his disciples; Sri Aurobindo used to write all night, answering the letters of his numerous disciples, and went practically blind as a result of his efforts. The worst part is that gurus have the power to see the disciples as they are, however the latter may try to disguise their thoughts and feelings. The Mother used to tell Satprem, her confidant, that every little vibration of doubt, ill-will, or negativity used to affect her body and that she had to constantly rectify the disharmony that was thus brought upon her. In the same way, one can observe that Guruji never complains, although he must be 'swallowing' hundreds of little miseries, nagging doubts, and petty demands every day.

Wherever Guruji stays, he plays the host and, invariably, throngs of people gather and want to meet him. They do so from morning till late at night. They experience a deep sense of belongingness in his presence, although everybody acts as if he or she 'owns' Guruji. Given the large flocks of people who come to meet him and given their diverse backgrounds, attitudes, and expectations, there is no dearth of bizarre and funny incidents. Someone may suddenly decide to stand up and dance, though there is not even enough sitting room! Sometimes people elbow others and push their way through to reach the front. People just feel free to be themselves around Sri Sri. On one occasion, Guruji was staying at an industrialist's place in Delhi and there was a volunteer who was controlling access to Guruji's room. An old lady, a little upset at having to wait, walked straight to the owner of the house, and gave him a tight slap for not letting her meet Guruji! Another time, a man who had lost his own house key while visiting Gurudev, felt free to rest in the owner's bed in the house, and when questioned by the owner, wanted to know who he was!

Vicky Block, an artist from Montreal, first met Sri Sri in 1987 and has since been a 'puzzled yet staunch' devotee. She has written two books on her years post-AOL (Art of Living), and they are hilarious. Here is what the experience of hosting Sri Sri is like: 'What does it feel like to have Sri Sri stay at your house? First you panic. Sri Sri hasn't arrived yet – but the possibility of people tearing around all over your place is more than you can think about, so you just don't. If you are the type of person who never answers the phone, likes to disappear into silence for days, and prefers to see friends away from your "territory" you might ask yourself what you are doing this for in the first place. The answer to that is that you have no idea. When Sri Sri arrives, so does the rest of the world. Now you have people milling around the kitchen asking for utensils that you have never heard of. There are people ironing, practising the guitar, meditating, and waiting to see Guruji. You are so uncomfortable the first day that you go up the street to a friend's apartment to use the shower. You come in wild-eyed, saying all kinds of things like not only

"Why are there people all over the house?" but "What am I doing with my life?" You don't believe in any of this stuff. You settle down in a soft chair and remark on how calm and quiet it is there. In less than two minutes, you jump up again, and say you have to go home in case you miss something. This is when you realize that the rest of the world has ceased to exist! After Guruji leaves, and when it is all over, I won't say you miss it. But there's a peculiar quality to the silence, a quality that wasn't there before. The house is very light and everything looks so bright, even the things that are still falling out of the cupboards. Having Sri Sri stay in your house doesn't make you better organized or more sociable. But in some imperceptible way, it changes everything. Having Sri Sri stay in your house is heaven and hell – and I'd do it again in a minute!'

In fact, Sri Sri himself is an excellent host. While attending International Advanced Courses, I have seen him take personal care, down to the minute details, of each one of the participants, making them comfortable and at home. He makes sure that even the drivers and watchmen are not neglected and are taken good care of. Once, there was a Westerner craving for brown bread though he never told anybody about it. Suddenly, he was delivered a loaf of brown bread by an ashram boy from Guruji's kutir. It's not only householders who come to see Guruji but also, often, saffron-clad saints, Christian priests and nuns, Muslim leaders, Buddhist and Jain monks, and wise men from other faiths come to seek guidance from him. In the time that I have spent with him, I have seen him totally at ease with a wide spectrum of people. The slum dweller connects with him as easily and effortlessly as the heads of India's largest business houses. He can animatedly discuss an agricultural method with a villager, just as easily as he can share his views on issues of national and international importance with political leaders. A keen learner, he often engages himself in a topical conversation with scientists, as effortlessly as he plays with a child.

The sheer variety that is packed into one day (invariably long) in the life of Guruji is mind-boggling, as narrated to me by Vinod Kumar: 'I once spent a full day with Sri Sri in Rishikesh and his schedule was packed to the minute. He began the day leading the Advanced Course participants and teachers in meditation at 5 a.m. He then interacted with a few of the participants and teachers and then went out to meet with some of the saints who live on [the banks of] the Ganges. He returned to the Vanprastha Ashram to talk to the parents of some Art of Living teachers. Following this, he was scheduled to address a gathering of CEOs, directors, and vice-presidents [of] one of the largest corporate houses of India. They had sent a fancy car to drive Sri Sri to the venue of the conference and back. On our return, Sri Sri made the car stop on the banks of the river opposite the ashram, saying that he would save 20 minutes if he simply walked across the bridge (Ram Jhula). To reach it by car was a roundabout drive. I was with him and we were walking briskly when suddenly he changed direction and dashed towards a cow that was eating a plastic bag! In the middle of a brisk walk on a packed day, how did he notice that? He pulled the plastic bag out of the cow's mouth, probably saving its life. Meanwhile, I offered to buy some mineral water for him to wash his hands, but he declined and continued to walk in the opposite direction holding the plastic bag. I followed, not knowing what would come next. He had spotted a garbage bin earlier!

After disposing of the plastic bag, he washed his hands in the Ganges and we proceeded to the bridge. There he saw a teenager struggling to push a cart carrying a few sacks of coal up the slope of the bridge. He realized that the boy was drunk. The next moment, Sri Sri was pushing the cart along with the boy, till the middle of the bridge. The bridge sloped downwards and we thought from there on, it would be easy for the boy. When he noticed that the boy was still unsteady on his feet, he asked one of the passers-by to ensure that the boy reached home safely! As he walked down further, a crowd collected around him, including some beggars. I began acting like a bodyguard and attempted to shoo them away, but Sri Sri stopped me. While he was walking with them, he answered their queries and reached the ashram just in time for his next meeting – with a group of prominent social activists and our Yuvacharyas (youth volunteers who are implementing Sri Sri's 5H programme in the villages of India'; see Chapter 8).

The Fun-filled Master

Of course, Guruji is fun, lots of fun. Being with him is entertaining, divine, imaginative, and unmitigated fun. Sri Sri loves fun and, in fact, one of his mottos is 'LSD': Laugh, Sing and Dance, a dig at those who prefer the artificial joys of chemical drugs. A greater part of all his courses are devoted to fun: laughing sessions, dancing with music, entertaining techniques. Guruji himself can be like a child: he wears funny hats offered by his devotees, with no thought about his 'image' of a serious guru; he gleefully sprays people with rubberized foam; or sprinkles 'holy' water on all during Navaratri. I find his simplicity and lack of airs extremely appealing and authentic.

In the ashram, as elsewhere, he attracts children like the legendary Pied Piper. In other spiritual places or places of contemplation and introspection, children are often not allowed entry, and even if they are, they are most definitely kept away from the spiritual head and formal assemblies. Not so with Sri Sri. I have seen children clamber up to the dais where he is seated delivering an interesting talk, and, in their innocence, offering him a flower, garland or a gift. He accepts them without a trace of irritation or impatience and continues as though nothing has happened.

Let me recount another incident in this context. There was this lady in the audience who would laugh out loudly at regular intervals for no apparent reason, so much so that Guruji would not be able to continue with his talk. People in the audience wondered why she was allowed in the satsang at all, and she was seen as a nuisance by a majority of them. But Sri Sri did not allow the resentment to grow and very skilfully brought the entire audience to enjoy her laughter and laugh along with her! Not only did the audience become more accepting of her behaviour, but also the lady in question learnt to appreciate the sensitivities of those around her. Thus, he teaches lessons without actually 'teaching' them! This is a phrase I have often heard from people who have interacted with Sri Sri – that they were made aware of their mistakes often without having to suffer the guilt of having committed an error!

Another favourite prank of Sri Sri is setting off the alarms at airports while going through the security check – the beep will go on repeatedly as Sri Sri passes through the metal detector frames, but no evidence of metal on his person will be found. He then sports his trademark mischievous smile, while the security personnel have confused looks on their faces.

In all major programmes, the organizers would have planned out things to the minutest detail, but Sri Sri would evidently create chaos. Once in Mumbai, there was a crowd of 50,000 people attending the satsang with Sri Sri and elaborate security arrangements were made. Even as the satsang was in full swing, Sri Sri simply jumped over the fence into the audience. The delighted crowd cheered, while the security personnel and the organizers perspired!

Sometimes, watching Sri Sri defies all your concepts of how a typical guru should be. He looks like an amalgamation of childishness and wisdom, dignity and mischievousness. A greater part of all his courses are thoroughly entertaining, and you experience a blend of profound wisdom and gaiety in an atmosphere of fun. 'Laugh and make others laugh; don't get entangled, and don't entangle others' is among his most popular quotes. During satsangs, he fires water guns on unsuspecting people, showers candies, and sprays celebration foam strings without being self-conscious at all or concerned about his 'image'.

The Baffling Guru

Sri Sri is so special as a Master because he works on you without your knowing it, so that your growth is effortless. In another of her very whacky books, titled *Now What*, Vicky writes: 'Someone once was arguing with Sri Sri about chanting in Sanskrit when we didn't know what the words meant. How can they have an effect on us if we don't know what they mean? Words are just words and they don't really do anything.

Sri Sri then calmly started to insult him, calling him a stupid fool and an idiot. The guy got very upset. "See," said Sri Sri, "look at the effect those words had on you. How can you say words have no real meaning? And those are ordinary words. How do you know the subtle influence of something as ancient and sacred as Sanskrit?"'

Another of Sri Sri's games is to put the wrong people in charge of things. Is this for our growth, or is Guruji a bad manager? Are these just incidental details far below the level of cosmic interest, or is this some kind of test? If someone is good at something, it will be the last thing he or she would be asked to do, or if that person is put in charge of a project, he or she would be overruled by someone who doesn't have any experience in that area. New levels of mismanagement are achieved, feelings are hurt, egos and friendships get squelched but still amazing things are accomplished.

On Sri Sri's special style of managing, Vicky comments: 'Part of the problem appears to be that Sri Sri specializes in games like putting someone in a position of responsibility without giving them the authority to do anything except fend off complaints, saying: "Look this is the way it has been decided by the committee, and there is nothing I can do." While such persons are spending all of their time holding back the tidal wave of disruption and advice, some zealot has the nerve to sneak behind them, and ignoring all the rules and hierarchy, actually DO the job whether they have the qualifications or not.'

Marielle, another American devotee of Sri Sri, recalls that once, when visiting India, her typewriter suddenly refused to type certain letters. Getting anything fixed in India was a problem. First, she asked Sri Sri. He jokingly said Shiva was responsible for it. So after the Shiva puja the next morning, she took an orange chrysanthemum, put it on the keys of her typewriter, and shut her door so no one would hear her. 'Listen Shiva,' she said, 'I don't know how to pray to you properly, but if you are responsible for breaking my typewriter, please fix it. At least, give me a sign.' She reasoned with Shiva for a little while, and then was just about to put in a piece of paper to see if anything had changed, when a disciple called Serjit came in. He had obviously heard her last prayer and glowered at the flower on the keys. 'What do you think you're doing?' he said grabbing it. 'Don't you know that's exactly what is wrong with this country? For centuries people have been praying to gods for this and that without taking responsibility for anything. If you want something to happen, you have to take action.' Marielle decided that this was the necessary sign from Shiva and took her typewriter into town to get it fixed.

Sometimes people come and bother Guruji with very trivial issues like, 'my cat is sick', 'I am going shopping, please bless me so that I do it well', 'what should I name my son or daughter' and so on. Once, as I was getting irritated by all these silly matters, Guruji looked at me and remarked: 'Tolerating ignorance is the last tapasya (penance).' Indeed, from the very beginning, I observed that my doubts and prejudices seemed to make no difference to him and the way in which he treated me. There was total acceptance and love on Sri Sri's part, as though he was deliberately giving me the space I required for my doubts to be cleared. He was only concerned about my comfort and well-being. Initially, it was hard to digest, but time proved otherwise. I was to discover later that he dealt with everyone the same way – with unconditional love.

The Caring Guru

Talking to people who have been associated with Sri Sri for even a short period, one comes to know that he is committed 100 per cent to whatever he does. Here are a few testimonies from teachers and disciples.

Philip mentions an instance when a cat came meowing outside his door, just as Sri Sri was about to have his food. Immediately, he set aside some rice on a plate to be given to the cat. As Philip was about to pick up the plate, he stopped him, saying that the rice was too hot and the cat would burn its tongue. He then poured some yoghurt on the rice to cool it down, and added some vegetables, after ensuring that they were not too spicy for the feline!

Vinod relates a recent episode that took place in Lithuania, where, during the course of a public talk, Sri Sri had said in response to a question about his message for children: 'Leave a better world for them than the way we found it.' The next morning, Sri Sri was slightly late in reaching the car they had to take to get to the airport. When asked what had delayed him, Sri Sri replied, 'I got a little busy cleaning my room'. It struck Vinod then that this was exactly what Sri Sri had spoken about the day before – leaving things better than you found them.

The depth of Sri Sri's silence, says Bindiya Jain, a close disciple, is mirrored in the dynamic activity around him. He not only inspires people to act, but he himself works tirelessly without getting stressed. Aware that his assistants cannot cope with his speed, he works them in rotation. If you have any doubts about his energy level and capacity, you just need to travel with him for a few days – the doubts will simply vanish. He is at once serene, and alert and active too: he plunges into situations of conflict, and changes the atmosphere to one of harmony. He enjoys cooking, and once in a while, he surprises people by coming up with an elaborate meal for them. He loves gardening too.

During the Kumbh Mela at Haridwar (a place of pilgrimage in Uttarakhand where the river Ganga enters the plains), remembers Bindiya, Guruji's black bag carrying his passport and other travel documents was found to be missing. Nitin, who was carrying the bag, had left it on top of a car and forgot to pick it up while leaving. Since Guruji was scheduled to travel to Europe in ten days' time, it was important that the bag be located as soon as possible. Despite the best efforts of his disciples, however, the bag was not found. Through all this, Guruji did not make Nitin, as well as two others, Sood and Gary (who were with Nitin) feel guilty even for a moment. Everybody was getting frantic, but Sri Sri stated calmly: 'Relax and everything will be okay.' At that very moment a phone call came from the person who had found the bag and wanted to return it to the owner. (Guruji had earlier remarked that some angel would find the bag prior to his departure.) Most of us would have been agitated and would have blamed the person who lost our belongings as being irresponsible. Instead, initially tranquillity prevailed and later there was a celebration.

In death as in life, there is also celebration. Shagun, the mother of Neelu (an AOL teacher), who was also a teacher, passed away in an accident. Doubt arose in the minds of many of Sri Sri's disciples: 'How could this happen to someone who is devoted and on the path?' When questioned, Guruji replied: 'There is no distinction in the Divine as "mine", or "not mine", or to save someone and not to save others. Everybody belongs to the Divine, whether they are on the path or not.' Spurred by this statement, the bereaved family came out of their sorrow and joined the celebration. Everyone sang 'Jai Jai Radha Raman', the last bhajan sung during satsangs. One hug from Guruji and it was as though their sorrows had diminished. Guruji's hug has magical qualities in all those moments. As a child remarked, 'it felt like rainbows' when he got a hug at a satsang.

In 1998, during Holi (the flamboyant festival of colours that usually comes in March), he played with gusto and hugged all the 8000 people who had assembled at the celebration venue. Since then the crowds have become bigger and, in some states, where up to 300,000 people congregate, he has started moving amongst the crowds showering rose petals.

In the spring of 1987, Guruji was addressing a gathering of youth at Jhansi (in Uttar Pradesh). After his address, he was scheduled to board a train for Indore (in Madhya Pradesh) where Indu Jain (the chairperson of the *Times of India* group and a renowned spiritualist) had organized, through her contacts, a course for two hundred couples from business houses. Upon reaching the railway station, to the dismay of all present, Guruji decided to go to Delhi instead. It had so happened that a young devotee called Choka Reddy, an extraordinarily brilliant student from the Pusa Institute (New Delhi) who had recently done the Basic Course, had developed serious psychological problems, as he had attempted too many types of meditation. He had been admitted to a hospital where electric shocks, sedatives, and medication could not calm him down. Nobody could control his insanity and everybody prayed for a miracle. As soon as Guruji arrived in Delhi, he went straight to the hospital and held Choka's hand and immediately the boy's violent mood subsided. He started taking food and soon returned to normalcy. Today, he is working in the Agricultural University at Hyderabad.

We also heard that Guruji once went to Basel, Switzerland, to give a talk to one person! The story goes that he was double booked in France and Switzerland on the same day. Knowing that the event in France was bigger, he sent Eberhart and Urmila there and chose to go to Basel where the organizer, for some reason had cancelled the talk, at the last moment. There was only one person in the big hall, other than the four people who accompanied Guruji! They all sat in silence, greeted that one person and came home. That lone spectator, whose name is Marcel, is now an AOL teacher. A musician by profession, he still fondly remembers how Guruji came to meet him, instead of turning his attention towards a lecture for 300 people!

The Guru Who Loves to Celebrate

On one occasion, Guruji composed a new song for birthdays. According to him, a birthday is the day when a wave remembers its source, the ocean, and gains the dignity of the ocean. An individual soul with name and form remembers its true nature, as infinity beyond name and form. This is the song:

Today is the day the wave remembers
the ocean where it was born
And today is the day we all remember
that this world is our very own.

Happy birthday to you (2)
We belong to you
Happy birthday to — (name)
We all are your very own
Yes, we all are your very own.

Birthdays are celebrated with buntings, balloons, and garlands all over, and Guruji cuts the cake and throws pieces of it towards everybody, declaring: 'The cake is going to come flying to you!' Winking, he adds: 'If any swami sees me doing this, he may ostracize me.' I have never heard him utter the words 'I love you', but whenever people say that to him, he replies: 'Me too!'

During Christmas and Easter celebrations, he is mostly in Europe. There, he enjoys Christmas carols and songs in all European languages and has been known to hum a couple of Polish tunes. He is fond of a Taiwanese song as well. Once, even the Chinese New Year was celebrated at the Bangalore ashram, with a traditional deity in place. Guruji loves diversity and he urges people to maintain the wide variety of culture and tradition that India has been blessed with. He is thus deeply concerned about religious conversions in Northeast India, where the inhabitants are fast forgetting their tribal culture. He asserts that the loss of tribal culture is a loss to world heritage. His slogan is: 'Deepen the roots and broaden the vision.' That is why he wants the tribals to progress in modern thinking, but at the same time value their ancient traditions. For this purpose, he has opened around a hundred charitable schools in tribal areas. It was during the search for a suitable location in a remote area for one of these schools that he lost two of his dear disciples, Nandita and Nityanand, in an accident. There was an unmistakable sign of pain in his eyes when he was told about this accident, yet he managed to make the whole atmosphere lighter.

The Management Guru

The Art of Living course is now taught in over 130 countries and the Art of Living Foundation is now the largest NGO in the world. It has seen a phenomenal expansion only in the last decade or so, considering that Sri Sri did not allow any publicity for his courses and meetings till 1995. The foundation now comprises hundreds of Art of Living teachers, thousands of organizers, and millions of followers. I am sure modern-day organizations would be eager to know the secret behind its growth. How does the organization work? What is Sri Sri's management style? Sri Sri has been involved in a regimented organization long enough to know its drawbacks. In his own words: 'An organization should be like a picture frame. The frame should not eat away the picture.' In other words, just as without a frame it is not possible to hold a picture, without an organization, any work, whether spiritual or social, cannot happen. At the same time, if the organization becomes too regimented, it is like the frame eating the picture away. Thus, Sri Sri's organization has a loose structure, which allows a lot of freedom and creativity, and Sri Sri's attention is immediately drawn to any flaw in its working. This organizational structure can prove to be a very good model for the corporate sector because work happens not through motivation, but by inspiration. Sri Sri often encourages people to take up leadership roles and not just remain followers, so that they can become aware of their abilities. Though sometimes this situation creates chaos, he loves it because, as he says, 'chaos creates bliss'. Through all this you never see him get angry; he does all his mischief with a smile!

In India hundreds of thousands of people come to his satsangs, and the way they are organized is simply amazing. For example, over 300,000 people gathered in Surat (Gujarat) on 26 February 2001, over 200,000 in Ahmedabad (Gujarat) on 28 February 2000, and over 400,000 in Cochin (Kerala) on 17 February 2002. In Kerala, he addressed close to a million people over a period of five days. I was fortunate to travel with him in that state and see for myself the amount of devotion among those folks. Though there may have been internal squabbling and ego trips, with one and all vying for the attention of Sri Sri, once he is there, it seems as though all the differences have dissolved. Once he addressed the Kerala volunteers, numbering over 2500, at the end of a hectic day's work. When he asked them if they were tired, the answer was a deafening 'NO!' And I could see that their faces were really filled with joy, even after having worked so hard.

Are this boundless enthusiasm and this unconditional acceptance of the guru a reflection of an Indian mindset? Westerners are more organized, more rational, and more sceptical – maybe such a thing wouldn't work in the West. Such arguments roiled my mind till I went to Germany with Sri Sri on New Year 2002. Here, too, Sri Sri spent most of his time focusing on individual problems, listening with enormous patience to an old lady talking about her arthritis or parents about their children or ... the list is endless. When one gentleman kept pestering him, during the darshan line (a time when Sri Sri meets everybody in the ashram), Sri Sri responded, with firmness and compassion but without even a trace of frustration or irritation in voice or manner: 'I know, you have already asked the same question eight times today.' Another reason for the smooth functioning of Sri Sri's organization generally is that nobody seems to be afraid of making mistakes. I wonder if it is a cultural thing. Is it the same everywhere? It could well be, but here it is very obvious.

One big problem that arises whenever Sri Sri visits any place is: where will he stay? Another issue is: who will drive his vehicle? Many friends become enemies just on this issue. All the selfless service aspects disappear and selfishness rules when it comes to housing Sri Sri and cooking his food. Another rather unusual aspect of Sri Sri is that he refuses to accept huge sums as donations from the affluent, whereas he readily accepts small amounts from poor persons in order to make them feel a part of the organization and to instil in them a sense of self-pride.

Though it is a mass movement, the growth of the individual is not sidelined. Sri Sri often says: 'If individuals become strong and brilliant, then the society will become divine.' Like everywhere else, there are workaholics in the Art of Living too, but Sri Sri keeps them in check: for example, our friend Kishore, who likes to do everything perfectly and ahead of time! Of course, the organization goes crazy sometimes, but still you hardly come across any stress. I often wonder what makes people stay awake and work late at night with such cheerfulness. Sri Sri does not set goals or deadlines for people, yet the enthusiasm that I see in the volunteers, teachers, and organizers is unparalleled. At the end of it all, there is tremendous progress both for the individual and the organization.

In the AOL movement, the organizers get no benefits, monetary or otherwise, except perhaps some small recognition for their endeavours. However, they definitely experience the joy of doing something for Sri Sri. As I have said before, Guruji seems to be a bad manager for he often creates a good deal of chaos and seems to give certain jobs to people who are not very efficient. To him all important and serious jobs are also like training workshops. He is more interested in the growth of an individual. Unlike in many organizations there is no hierarchy – at least not a visible one – and confusion often reigns in all departments, from the housing to the publication section. You ask anybody anything and they reply, using Guruji's words: 'Relax and everything will be taken care of' or 'present moment is inevitable'. You only get more irritated. This methodology, if tried out in any corporate sector, could be very risky; but somehow it seems to work here, as the individual becomes strong and the organization is growing by leaps and bounds. It is interesting to see how orderliness actually springs out of this chaos.

The Compassionate Guru

This book is not about whitewashing the Art of Living and making everybody look perfect. In their feverishness to be around Sri Sri, it is not uncommon for people to forget all his teachings. A few of his teachers often elbow others aside, so as to be able to walk next to him. Some of his closest disciples will follow him right to his bathroom door and will sit virtually glued to him late into the night, till they are shooed out by one of his attendants. In their overwhelming need to be with him at all times, people forget all decency and consideration not only towards each other, but even towards him – never letting him alone, never giving him any rest, taxing him all the time, for a look, a pranam (salutation), a hug, or just to garland him endlessly. Thus, often Guruji has to ask to be locked inside his own kutir, so that people think he has gone out! Some of the teachers, in their zeal to do more courses, or get more applicants, fall into the trap of overselling their guru and indulge in too glib a marketing technique: putting-up huge posters of Sri Sri or hoardings of his photos, which are in bad taste (and of which he disapproves). But somehow, Sri Sri does not seem disturbed by any such development. His first principle of 'accept people as they are' comes through so clearly in the organization. As he once said: 'The Art of Living Course is just what life is.'

Chapter Eight

The Steps That Speak

...The pituitary gland has a connection to the hypothalamus gland, which is the seat of consciousness, our mind. Thousands of years ago, people had stated that [the] focus of [the] pituitary gland can affect the whole nervous system in a very positive way. Consciousness works through glands and cleans and brings energy into the immune system, strengthens it and keeps one healthy – 'Swastha'. 'Swastha' *means stabilized in one's self. Health means: mind is centred, focused, free of disturbances and solid.*

What attracted me most to Sri Sri Ravi Shankar, as I got to know him better, is 'the fact that he is a 'doing' guru, one who practises what he preaches. This quality is especially admirable in a country where people are quite passive, and spirituality has often become so divorced from the material, that the physical body of India, its social system, and political system have been left to rot and degenerate. It seems to me that Guruji has come to reform India and to send forth its radiance to the world. For this purpose, of course, he needs to tackle certain essential features of Indian life that are dragging this wonderful country, the spiritual light of this planet, towards self-destruction.

What struck me the first time I went to the Bangalore ashram was that there were only a few servants around and it was the sadhaks (volunteers) and inmates who did most of the jobs themselves, including cooking and even cleaning. Some of the guest rooms, personally cleaned and arranged by young ashramites, and tastefully decorated with candles, incense sticks, and photos of Guruji, are worth seeing. The whole ashram organization has been taken over, under Guruji's supervision, by these young ashramites and every time we go there, which is pretty often, there is some improvement: a rocky path has been paved, tiles have been laid somewhere, the place for washing utensils extended, landscaping done (Hi, Hannah and James!). Lots of young boys and girls, who come from affluent families, are thus encouraged to do things for themselves. And so, when they return to society, they bring back a different attitude, which goes further towards changing the system. This is the base India needs in order to reconstruct a healthy and just social system.

The Western world has a few favourite topics to whip India with, one being the caste system. It is true that this system is one of the factors that led to India's downfall as a great civilization. Yet, once upon a time, whatever India's detractors may say, the caste system was a remarkable set-up. As many sages have pointed out, caste was originally an arrangement for the distribution of functions in society, just as much as class in Europe, but the principle on which this distribution was based was peculiar to India. A Brahmin was a Brahmin not by mere birth, but because he discharged the duty of preserving the spiritual and intellectual elevation of the race, and he had to cultivate the spiritual temperament and acquire the spiritual training, which alone would qualify him for the task. And so it was for the Kshatriya (warrior), who defended his country, the Vaishya (trader or businessman), who gave it prosperity, and the Shudra, who discharged the humbler tasks without which the other castes could not perform their share of labour for the common good. Nevertheless, as Sri Aurobindo pointed out, 'the spirit of caste arrogance, exclusiveness and superiority came to dominate it instead of the spirit of duty, and the change weakened the nation and helped to reduce it to its present condition'. This is where Sri Sri intervenes again: not only is there no caste, religion or ethnic bar in the Art of Living, which makes it a casteless movement (a direction India would do well to take), but also Guruji has tried to counterbalance this constant harping on the 'oppressed Dalits' by Christian missionaries and Marxist scholars. He has published a book on Dalits, which shows that many of India's revered saints, gurus and Gods (such as Krishna) were from the so-called 'lower castes'. In a new Indian society, Brahmins, not by birth but by choice, will continue to serve the spiritual and the religious; the Kshatriyas will be the professional soldiers, voluntarily, as it happens anyway today; there always will be Vaishyas in any society – and business nowadays seems to be the option of many; and the caste of Shudras will slowly disappear, as has happened in the West, where there are few servants left, and be replaced by a better-paid casteless professional 'help'.

While travelling in different parts of India, I am pained to observe at what is being done to the physical body of this great country: India's ecological condition is catastrophic. Many experts have warned that, by the middle of this century, there will be no more forest cover left here. Already, hardly 11 per cent of India's classified forests have adequate density, whereas in 1950, one third of India's total area was still forested. Each year India loses, through deforestation, a territory bigger than France, that is, nearly 2 million hectares. Of this territory, only 3 per cent is protected – and even that little portion is in danger, because of population pressure, big dams (like the Sardar Sarovar on the river Narmada), and widespread industrialization. India's population is expected to cross the billion-and-a-half mark by 2050 unless drastic measures are taken, and will spill over everywhere, stifling any progress and undoing all gains. India's cities will be so polluted by the industries within them apart from the exhaust fumes from millions of vehicles that it will be impossible to breathe any more; its rivers will be so poisoned by industrial effluents that all forms of life will have long disappeared from them. There will be no drinking water left, except imported mineral water. And India will be littered with so much plastic – bags, bottles, buckets – that it will be practically impossible to ever get rid of them.

Sri Sri shows great concern for ecology and the environment, i.e., for India's physical body: no plastic bags in his ashram; discarded food and other waste material are used to make compost; and all other trash is sorted out and recycled, wherever possible, in different pits. There have been other positive developments as well: solar energy is slowly being introduced; trees have been planted by the thousands; and reverse osmosis is used for water generation. In the ashram, the food is vegetarian and served fresh. Recently, when the Karnataka Government was planning to enlarge the Kanakapura road, where the ashram is situated, hundreds of trees – tamarind, peepul (banyan), neem (*Azadirachta indica*), some of them more than a hundred years old – bordering the road were to be chopped down. Guruji's disciples swung into action: they began writing petitions to the powers that be, meeting officials, and organizing protests in various places. Will their efforts save the trees? That's another question altogether. We in Auroville fought against the enlargement of the Chennai–Mahabalipuram–Pondicherry road, now called the East Coast Road, but we could not save hundreds of ancient and valuable trees, in spite of going to court. The only concession we were allowed was to replant saplings on the side of the new road. Ten years later, the new trees are already

Sri Sri in the arms of his mother

Sri Sri acknowledging the greetings of his devotees

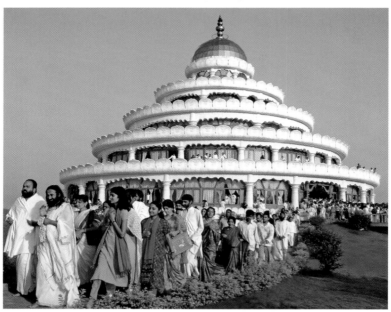

Sri Sri and his devotees at the ashram

Sri Sri in a joyful mood

Sri Sri taking a stroll amidst nature

Thousands greet The Guru of Joy wherever he goes

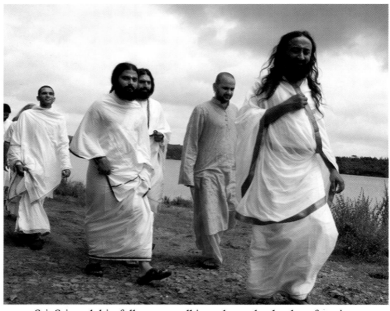

Sri Sri and his followers walking along the banks of a river

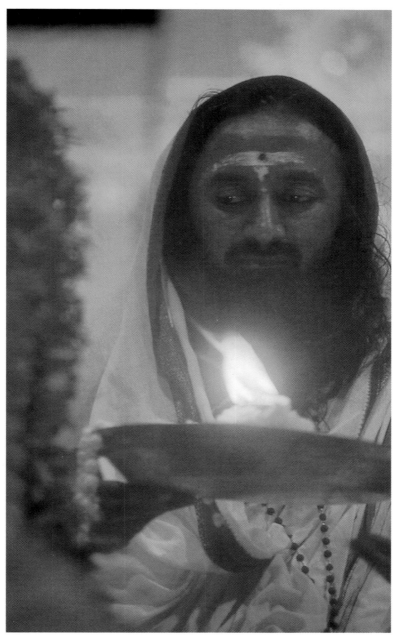

Sri Sri doing *aarti:* rediscovering the inner meaning of the art of puja

Sri Sri performing a puja in Kolkatta

Sri Sri in a moment of celebration

Sri Sri engrossed in meditation

Thousands doing The Mahakriya in Kerala

Guruji in meditation

The ancient and the new come together

providing much-needed shade, a tribute to nature's never-ending goodwill. Unfortunately, we heard recently that the government is planning to enlarge the road once more ... but a good guru is one who never gives up!

One of the greatest advantages for Guruji is that he knows many Indian languages and communicates well with people from both North India and South India. In the West, the Church has played a major part both socially and politically. But in India, people hold the belief that spiritual Masters should have no role in national politics. Nevertheless, Sri Sri has mature and well-thought-out ideas and views about politics and some of his advice to political leaders has been greatly valued. He asks people around him to read out worthwhile articles to him from newspapers and magazines while he is travelling or when his schedule permits. He also keeps in touch with current affairs and important events taking place in the world and airs his anxiety on subjects such as violence, corruption, politics, and religion. One aspect that has really concerned him is religious conversions. He has spoken brilliantly in many forums on current issues and topics. Concerned with the decline in positive and constructive journalism in India, he inspired some senior journalists to come together and start the Sri Sri Centre for Media Studies.

Yet, it is also true that he keeps his distance from politics. This is very unfortunate, as Sri Sri could work wonders in the political system of India with his huge following. I sometimes wonder why he refrains from influencing a political system that is so corrupt and criminalized, with every party playing vote-bank politics. Why does he not also deal with the media, which is so biased against the Hindus and constantly tries to malign Indian gurus by calling them 'godmen'? It is also very sad that an aggressive religious conversion by the evangelists is going on at the moment, right under the nose of the Hindu saints, who seem to be oblivious to it. In such situations, the activist in me becomes very restless.

But every time I bring up the subject with Sri Sri, he simply smiles or changes the topic. There are certain questions for which you can never get answers from him. It can be frustrating at times and at other times it allows you to see something beyond – maybe it relates to some metaphysical factor. There are many fanatics who interpret every little move of his and attribute them to some cosmic reason. I am not one of them. And when such questions dog your mind, as often happens in my case, I just stop bothering. As he once responded to someone who was pestering him with the same question again and again: 'Asking a question is your right and answering it or not is mine.' I do feel compassion for him. He is bombarded with questions and with what patience he listens to them! But my restless mind does not stop asking either. As if he knew my condition, he once came right up to me in the darshan line and asked me to listen to the Ashtavakra tapes, carrying the discourse he gave on the treatise by the Sage Ashtavakra, which beautifully explains the knowledge of the Self.

I went back to my room and decided to act upon his advice. Immediately, a certain quietness descended upon me. The cacophony of the frogs outside my room appeared musical and I started smiling to myself. It took me quite a few days to listen to the forty-one tapes on Ashtavakra, though, for they had to be heard in a group and then discussed. Everybody in the small group would put forth his or her opinion intensely and the discussions sometimes completely went off-track. But such interaction gave many opportunities to all of us to find out where each one was stuck. I had once heard Guruji saying that the mind was the most entertaining object we possess. If only we could watch it!

One of the criticisms about Sri Sri in the media is that he is a guru of 'the elite' and caters only to the rich. It is pointed out that he often travels in a Mercedes Benz or stays in the houses of his rich disciples. But little do they know that Guruji has actually no car of his own and that he used to travel in rickshaws, or as Kishore remembers, 'on the back of a scooter', and that he does not mind staying in any humble abode. And what about the crores of villagers, the illiterates, the poor and the sick who come for his blessings or receive the benefits of his many rural projects? A few of his rural projects and schemes for the deprived, the oppressed and the outcasts of society are now described.

Youth Training Programme

One night, while at Rishikesh, Sri Sri asked if it was anyone's birthday. Five people stood up. Amongst them I spotted a familiar face – it was Sanjay, a shy and reserved boy, whom I had earlier seen in the Bangalore ashram. Everyone was singing the Art of Living birthday song and Guruji garlanded all of them. The next day I saw Sanjay addressing a group of people – it was not the Sanjay I remembered. There was a striking difference in his demeanour. Gone was the timidity – it had been replaced by a confidence that shone on his face. I managed to speak to him around lunchtime and learnt that he had become a Yuvacharya (youth leader) after undergoing

Sri Sri's Youth Training Programme, perhaps the most ambitious scheme to educate the rural community. Like Sanjay, most Yuvacharyas are volunteers, inspired by Ravi Shankar to do service where it is the most needed: in rural and tribal areas. Another charitable trust, Sri Sri Vidya Mandir, has also been founded to spread education.

Here are comments of some of the people who have benefited from the programme:

'I was a totally pessimistic person who saw only negativity in everything around me. Depressed in life, I was suffering both physically and mentally. Unenthusiastically, I dragged myself around as the days and years passed. The YTP is the best thing that happened in my life. I think this is the most unique programme in the world. It has revolutionized my outlook from failure, sorrow, and stress to enthusiasm and dynamism. I feel incredibly strong,' says Sajda Rehman, a student from Jamshedpur (now in Jharkhand state). Ahinsa, another student from Surat, wrote: 'Before YTP I was like a kite whose thread has been snapped, drifting aimlessly in the sky. I lacked confidence and liked to stay aloof from the world around me. YTP has transformed my life completely. Now my life has a sense of commitment, responsibility, love, and patriotism. I feel strong and am ready to serve the people.'

Hanumantesh, a yoga teacher from Shimoga (Karnataka), declares: 'After my YTP Course, I realized that I had [earlier] restricted my life to only one area. Now I can reach farther to every corner of my country – India. YTP has strengthened my drive for service. I can now face any challenge whatsoever.'

Remember the devastating earthquake that hit many areas of the Indian subcontinent on 26 January 2001? The quake, measuring 7.9 on the Richter scale, with its epicentre around

20 km northeast of Bhuj in Gujarat, caused immense loss of life and property. The Art of Living Foundation utilized its grassroots approach to help the quake victims, organizing teams of volunteers from around the world, both on the ground and through the Internet. These NGO teams possessed the experience, network, and established centres of distribution in India to be invaluable in streamlining the initially chaotic relief efforts.

The 5H Programme

Sanjay also talked animatedly about the 5H (home, health, hygiene, harmony in diversity, and human values) programme. This programme, without doubt, is the star project of the Art of Living as an NGO and the vehicle through which the International Association for Human Values runs a wide array of humanitarian service projects in India as well as in other countries around the world. He explained to me that Sri Sri Ravi Shankar feels that human suffering has many faces. In some parts of the world, people live in squalor and abject poverty, without proper sanitation or housing. Unhygienic conditions and lack of proper education about health and hygiene give rise to disease, resulting in poor health. In other parts of the world, people may have achieved a decent standard of living, but we find dissension, disharmony, stress, violence, crime, and other social ills. In some countries, war has destroyed the social fabric and brought great suffering. There is a pressing need for healing at all levels. In each of these situations, the International Association for Human Values, through its 5H programme, assists in eradicating misery and in transforming society.

According to Guruji: 'Human life is a great and rare gift, and all people on this planet should have the chance to express through their lives the full potential of their humanness.' This means claiming their birthright to a disease-free body and a stress-free mind, which, in turn, means leading lives that express human values such as compassion, nonviolence, generosity, and an ethic of service and caring for all life. Thus, he feels that social transformation begins with a happy and healthy individual who has attained a decent standard of living and has received essential education in health, hygiene, and life skills. Addressing substandard housing and lack of sanitation alone can neither result in the long-term eradication of misery nor bring about a fundamental social transformation. Education is essential, particularly education in human values. Once the material conditions of living have reached an adequate level, there is a possibility for true humanness to be expressed in life. A sense of belonging, sharing, non-violence, caring for life, and caring for the planet are among the values that need to be nurtured. The development of human values is essential in creating loving and happy families, cohesive communities, and harmonious relations among all people and nations – all prerequisites for peace, harmony, and well-being on the planet. The five elements of the action plan are:

Health: The first step towards leading a happy, fulfilling life. Yet vast segments of the world's population do not have access to proper nutrition or medical and dental care, nor have they received even the most rudimentary education in achieving and maintaining good health. The 5H programme has already initiated projects in various areas of India, besides organizing healthcare camps, which provide medical and dental care to the rural population. Medical assistance has also been provided to children suffering from polio in a number of regions in Gujarat. The 5H programme's medium-term objectives are: broadening the areas of service, including expansion to other developing countries in Asia and Africa; setting up medical centres in various rural villages; providing ambulances for remote areas; and initiating alcohol/tobacco/drug deaddiction and rehabilitation programmes. Additionally, volunteers provide basic healthcare education.

Hygiene: Achieving and maintaining good health are difficult in areas where there are inadequate sanitation practices, a lack of clean drinking water, and insufficient means for garbage disposal. Many of the world's poor live in such deplorable conditions.

The 5H programme is currently addressing this situation in rural villages in India through the simple yet effective means of building toilets, digging bore wells for access to clean drinking water, constructing water storage tanks, and providing garbage bins where needed. Volunteers create awareness about hygiene among the rural population. This programme is being expanded to cover more regions of India as well as other developing countries in Asia and Africa.

Housing: Many of the world's poor are homeless, living on the streets or in substandard housing conditions. This serious problem is being addressed by the International Association for Human Values through its 'Homes for Change' initiative, under the 5H programme, which has built modest but durable homes for poor families, at no cost to them. Each home has a kitchen, a bedroom, a family room, and a toilet. All homes are built of durable brick and cement. Through 'Homes for Change', houses are presently being built for poor families in rural South India. This programme is being expanded to other countries as well. It costs approximately US $ 2000 to build one of these homes in India. Donors can contribute the cost of an entire house for a designated family, or they can contribute the cost of particular items, such as toilet, materials, or labour. All 5H projects are planned in consultation with the local population to ensure that the greatest needs of both individuals and the whole community are met.

Human values: There is a growing awareness that the long-term eradication of poverty and human misery requires a fundamental shift in consciousness. Many projects aimed at improving the material conditions of life for the poor have had disappointing long-term results and have been ineffective in eradicating the roots of poverty. The 5H programme provides a holistic ongoing framework of education and support that has the potential to lift people permanently out of the trap of poverty and misery. Human values are the hallmark of human evolution and the basis of a peaceful and prosperous world. These values can flourish once the basic material needs of a community have been met. Violence, hatred, crime, and other pervasive social ills are the direct result of a lack of attention to human values. The foundation for developing human values is a sense of belonging and oneness, which arises spontaneously through the participation of the whole community in the uplift of each of its members in the context of 5H projects. Life skills, educational programmes emphasizing values, as well as multiethnic festivals organized by volunteers also contribute to the development of a sense of belonging and an ethic of service, bringing cohesion to families and communities.

Harmony in diversity is the overall objective of the 5H programme. A number of projects that focus specifically on this objective proved useful in the war-torn regions of Eastern Europe. In the aftermath of armed conflict, there is a need to work with survivors to promote healing and restore harmony. The International Association for Human Values developed a volunteer programme, in collaboration with its partners, to respond to this pressing need in Croatia, Bosnia, and Kosovo. The programme provides an opportunity for volunteers to commit themselves for one year to help victims of war rebuild their lives and begin the process of emotional healing. Volunteers receive intensive training in teaching a carefully designed programme that promotes harmony and ensures healing. The volunteers also coordinate service projects to rebuild homes and provide clothing, in liaison with the International Association for Human Values. Sri Sri Ravi Shankar feels that ending violence in society is one of the greatest challenges in today's world. All forms of violence – youth violence, domestic violence, human rights violations, criminal behaviour, and war – spring from the same seed of hatred. How can hatred be eliminated? 'The present crisis,' says Guruji, 'is basically one of identification: How do people see their basic identity? What is their fundamental concept of who they are? Limited and fragmented identification leads to hatred, violence, and war.' The International Association for Human Values, in collaboration with its partners, provides educational programmes for all sectors of society aimed at bringing about this fundamental understanding, which is the basis of *harmony in diversity* and ultimately world peace.

These values have already been brought to over 8000 villages all over India through Nava Chetana Shivir, an awareness-enhancing programme, at the end of which the villagers take up service projects in their areas. Sri Sri takes intense interest in these programmes and devotes time to visit villages, monitor the progress of the programmes, and provide wise counsel. The ultimate goal is to create an India that is swachha (clean), swastha (healthy), sushikshita (educated), subhadra (auspicious), and sundara (beautiful).

Art of Living for Peace

I found that Sanjay was addressing a group of some other people the next evening, but I sensed a reluctance in him to talk to me about them. After some persistence, he agreed to speak, on condition that I keep everything confidential. The people he was addressing were members of ultra-left rival warring groups from Bihar: they were dreaded criminals. One woman had apparently committed 60 murders and two of the men over 250. I thought that these acts were impossible, despite the fact that these groups had been in the news for committing some of the biggest massacres in Bihar, the land where the Buddha – the apostle of peace – attained Enlightenment. I was wondering what they were doing in a meditation centre, and later found out that Sri Sri had taken the initiative to restore peace and bring about a transformation in the troubled land that is Bihar. I remembered also reading about the Sudarshan Kriya's effectiveness in conflict resolution and the UN initiative to use it in the Bosnian war.

Naturally, I felt that it must have taken a lot of persuasion and time to get them here, and asked Sanjay about his experience. He smiled and remarked that it took him six days – two days to reach Bihar, two to collect them, and two to return! Sanjay had visited Rishikesh ten days earlier with a plan to spend his birthday with Sri Sri. While at Rishikesh, he saw the news item about large-scale massacres in Bihar. Inspired by Sri Sri, he went to the heartland of the crime himself, and separately invited the warring factions to visit Rishikesh and meet Sri Sri. At first, the heads of the groups challenged Sanjay to reach the mainland without getting killed in the process – if he reached unharmed, they told him, they would admit that Sanjay's guru was worthy of their faith! Sanjay cheerfully agreed, and called them from Patna, the capital of Bihar, after reaching there safe and sound. They were so surprised at Sanjay's safe passage through the killing fields that they kept their word and agreed to come. Naturally, both the groups did not know about their rivals' coming. And when they first encountered each other face to face after arriving in Rishikesh, sparks flew. 'But', says Sanjay, 'Sri Sri's presence dissolved the conflict and they agreed to take the Art of Living Course together.' Over the next few days, the Sudarshan Kriya, meditation, and the atmosphere of celebration brought about a sea change in their attitude. At the end of their course, they voluntarily swore in Sri Sri's presence to give up violence and devote their time to service. Soon after returning, they sent a contingent of nearly 200 people to go through the same programme, which had a profound influence on them. It is with those groups that Sanjay was discussing strategies of how to go about performing the work in the villages.

Prisoners of Fortune

Sensing my keen interest in Bihar, and with the characteristic Indian quality of special consideration for a guest, Sanjay sent word for Indu Sinha, another teacher from Bihar, to meet us. Indu, a typical middle-aged Indian housewife, told me her story: She was born and raised in Bihar, and had always been saddened by the high criminal activity that went on there and by the number of prisoners that crowded Bihar's notoriously dangerous jails. Keen on making a difference, she took Sri Sri's blessings before approaching the superintendent of Bihar's largest jail and offering Prison SMART – Prison Stress Management and Rehabilitation Training – courses for the warring factions that were serving their sentence there. The superintendent, though initially sceptical, agreed to try it out, and what happened over the next few weeks was truly miraculous. The dreaded criminals, with histories of multiple murders, aired their hostilities aggressively to Indu on the first day of the six-day course. But by the third day, cleansed of their trauma by the Sudarshan Kriya, they would melt and cry. Many of them opened up and stated that although they had sworn to kill the people who put them in jail, they were now ready to let go of their past. The police force was so relieved that such an unexpected change of attitude had taken place in a place that was infamous for its many jailbreaks and gang wars that they threw open many other jails to the programme. All these developments culminated in Sri Sri's visit to the Patna Jail in May 2002.

The success achieved with Bihar criminals inspired the Bombay police to aggressively utilize the Prison SMART course in their jails as well. After taking two such courses, Mohammed Afroze, an alleged Al-Qaeda operative who was planning to blow up the London House of Commons, underwent a complete change of heart. Fellow prisoners found an aloof Afroze transformed into a definitely more friendly, cheerful and relaxed person. He himself commented that 'he was promised [that he would go] to heaven after death, but he had found heaven right here'. Later, he refused an offer to be released on bail, as he had enrolled for the Advanced Course in the jail soon thereafter. This news made headlines in most major Bombay newspapers.

I have heard Sri Sri say: 'Terrorists are basically good people, as they are willing to put their life behind their cause. They just need the right direction in life.' In fact, if you look carefully at Osama bin Laden's face in the photos, you can see an almost mystical expression. Subsequently, Sanjay told me that several thousand prisoners in New Delhi's Tihar Jail also took the Prison SMART course, culminating in a visit by Sri Sri there. During the visit, Sri Sri found that a large number of people over 60 years of age and physically weak were being held in captivity for alleged crimes. In spite of his extremely busy schedule, Sri Sri organized a survey of those people, and appealed for general mercy for them to the lieutenant governor of Delhi and sought their release.

It was well past lunchtime, and the warm sun had already begun its descent. Indu Sinha and Sanjay took their leave, as the young Raghavendra was briskly walking towards the amphitheatre to do a sound check for the evening satsang. It was a very still and serene moment. And I wondered to myself how, whatever be the field of activity – medicine, journalism, or chemical-free farming – Sri Sri was right there, encouraging everybody and giving them his full support. In my long journalistic career, I have seen quite a few social activists who rake up different issues and create frustration in order to achieve their results. I had often wondered if there was an alternative method of reform, without frustration, anger and dejection. I think I found it here – the approach of love. The old saying, 'Love is the greatest force of transformation', is naturally demonstrated here.

Chapter Nine

The Disciples

In presence of your Sadguru
knowledge flourishes, sorrow
diminishes; without any reason,
joy wells up, lack diminishes;
abundance dawns; and all talents manifest.
To the degree you feel connected
to your guru, these qualities
manifest in your life.

Sri Sri is a great guru, and he has great disciples. What is even more remarkable is that many of his disciples are young and talented. Not for Guruji an ashram with old and feeble sadhaks, but, on the contrary, many young, bright, luminous souls, whom he often picks up in his Art Excel courses, bringing them to maturity through subtle personal coaching. Eventually, many of these youngsters become teachers. Western disciples of Indian gurus have sometimes perfected the art of looking warm and good, while retaining a certain hardness inside. Or you have the other extreme, where people, both Western and Eastern, who have taken to the spiritual path tend to appear, after a certain age, dour and unsmiling, which is the result of the routine, however spiritualized it may be, and is a manifestation of self-satisfaction at being on the 'right' path. Not so with most of Sri Sri's Western disciples; although they do not always display the ease and transparency that come to Indians naturally, because of their spiritualized background, they possess genuine warmth, openness, generosity, and selflessness.

From PhDs to illiterates, from farmers to MTV VJs, from the slums of Dharavi (in Bombay) to the Silicon Valley, Sri Sri's disciples are as diverse as the human race itself. A fair number of them are professionals with degrees from the prestigious Indian Institutes of Technology (IITs) and Indian Institutes of Management (IIMs), and are typically from a middle-class background. There are a sizeable number of young people from all continents except Antarctica. Many of them did the Art of Living course while they were at college, and it touched them in a way all the other education in their life did not: It restored their confidence and enthusiasm, healed them of disorders, and gave a sense of direction in their lives. I know for a fact that Sri Sri spends a lot of personal time coaching, mentoring, and grooming his young devotees, and so do many of his senior teachers. These youngsters have seen their talents blossom forth in Sri Sri's presence – be it in poetry or music, or organizing, programming, and designing.

Curious to get a closer look at some of Sri Sri's young disciples and to understand them better, I approached Ajay Vig from Delhi, who was caught up in an animated discussion with Vinod in the administration block of the ashram, while waiting for a guest speaker to address the Youth Training Programme participants. Ajay is the coordinator for Sri Sri's Youth Training Programme under which, as we have seen earlier, rural youth gain vital leadership training to take up responsibility for their own progress. Ajay graduated from the IIM, Ahmedabad, which is as famous as the Harvard Business School. 'I heard Sri Sri talk about how India's development depended on the improvement of rural youth, as 70 per cent of India is in her villages,' he recalls. 'Sri Sri's presence inspired me to take up the cause of rural youth instead of just worrying about my bread and butter. I found my talents put to good use in these projects, and grew to become the coordinator of the Youth Leadership Training Programme (YLTP) which transforms unemployed or angry village youth into productive and confident people.' The bright sparks from the YLTP are then offered a four-month Sri Sri Rural Development Programme (SSRDP) headed by Vinod. This programme offers vocational training in the areas of carpentry, handling lathe machines, welding, organic farming, commercial transactions, and office management. Ajay explained that 'there is not so much dearth of employment in India as there is a dearth of employability. The skills of physical fitness, the right attitude and responsibility, initiative and action orientation coupled with office management and commercial skills make the SSRDP graduates highly employable.' Ajay further remarked that 'Sri Sri attends to the SSRDP team by paying attention to their growth and surprising them with new uniforms, gifts, sweets. Currently, the second batch of about 60 rural youth is taking this intensive programme.'

Sri Sri has also been a source of diverse experiences to his disciples. Hassan Helilian, for instance, was born in Iran, migrated to Canada and, as a taxi driver, had a bizarre experience with a customer who wished to travel 'long distance' with him in his taxi. He relates the episode as follows: 'After working all day, I picked up a customer in the early hours of the morning. He wanted to travel a long distance and wanted to make a deal with me for fifty dollars. I told him that it was not possible and that I would have to put the meter on. He agreed, but once we were on the highway, he started cursing me. Feeling the anger rise in me, I stopped the car. He was quiet for a moment and then, pulling out a gun, he said, "I can shoot you, kill you, don't mess with me!" For a moment I was petrified; I felt the beads of sweat on my forehead and the tightness in my chest. Then this strong feeling came over me that none could harm me, because wherever I go, I feel the presence of Guruji. I uttered a silent prayer. The man continued to scream at me, when suddenly his eyes fell on Guruji's picture on the dashboard. He started mumbling, then became quiet. After some moments he asked: "Who is this man?" I turned, looked straight into his eyes, and replied: "That is a picture of my guru." Suddenly he became mellow, folded his hands in "namaste", and bowed, first to the picture, then to me. He did this many times and kept saying "I'm sorry!" At the end of the journey, he not only paid me my full fare, but I also got a lavish tip!'

Another disciple from the US, Professor Katherine Kamanda, who is a PhD and whose subject is world religions, recalled that her mother had a vision of Sri Sri a day before she was born. 'My mother had a difficult pregnancy. She had been quite ill during most of it and had been in a car accident towards the end. In the last month of her pregnancy, she was confined to bed as the doctor was worried that I might not make it. Needless to say, my mother was overcome with fear, and could barely sleep because of her worries. Then, one night, a strange thing happened. She told me that the room filled with a golden light and a Being appeared before her. I have always heard her describe him as wearing a white, flowing robe, having long black hair and a beard. But the most beautiful thing about this Being, my mother would tell me, were his eyes. She said she had never seen such beautiful eyes in her entire life; he didn't say anything to her, but communicated the most exquisite love through those eyes. He just washed wave after wave of love over her with those eyes, removing her fear forever. She always said that she thought he might have been Jesus, but whoever he was, she would never forget him! She never again felt fear in her life … even to this day.

When I was 19 and in college, I met Guruji. My mother thought I had joined a cult and was worried about me. When I did my sadhana [means or path of attaining the spiritual goal], she would hear strange noises coming from my room and wondered who the saint with the long hair and beard in the picture placed with reverence on my shrine was, though she would never actually look at it. Then came the day when she was diagnosed [as having] cancer. She wanted to know who my guru was, what he taught me, and what he looked like. When I showed his photo to her, she gazed into his eyes and began to cry. I asked her what was wrong and she answered: "This is the man who came to me the night before you were born!"'

Michael Adams, an American priest, 'felt the presence of Christ in Sri Sri during his first encounter'. Subsequently, he wrote to Sri Sri: 'Dearest Gurudev, as a priest, I see you at the altar. I have chosen to see you as the living Christ, and I imagine that those who saw Jesus must have experienced him just as we experience you now. I always see you at the altar and ask Your blessings and presence in my masses. God, guru, and self are indeed all the same, yet guru is still so special for guru is God in a body. We are blessed and thankful to have your love. I ask for your continued blessings in my life, in all my roles, that I may be blessed and grow to become nobody and then to become everybody. I wish to live in bliss and share it with others, bless and love others with the strength and unity of God, guru, and self in realization. You are as close as my heart. But I want more! I want nothing less than to be you!'

Manju Kishinchand from Indonesia overcame her bulimia through the grace of Sri Sri and qualified to become an MTV

VJ. As she puts it: 'I still remember those days when I was preparing myself to be an MTV VJ. Physically, it was taking its toll. I abused my body, and the desire to fit into the MTV image of a perfect slim personality made me go on various diets and spend hours in the gym. As a result I often fell sick, was admitted to the hospital, and frequently the doctors had to give large doses of antibiotics as my immune system had completely given up. Then I met Guruji and spent some time at the ashram. It is funny but very few people know what actually goes on in the minds of people who are going through bulimia – the person's mind would be thinking about food and body all through the day and dreaming about it too. It is a disease that completely wrecks one's mind and of course, one's body. Guruji advised me patiently about my eating habits. He inquired about the functioning of my stomach, and would actually tell me what to do next and how. How the Kriya and all the other cleansing processes kept me going, only I know, because on the outside I looked very healthy and beautiful. Before meeting Gurudev, life was an effort, now it is effortless. If a fish is asked to narrate the vastness of an ocean or to describe its greatness, what can it say?'

Iravati Kulkarni, a Sanskrit graduate and singer from Pune (in Maharashtra, earlier spelt as Poona) considers Sri Sri to be her friend, philosopher, and guide. She recounts some remarkable anecdotes: 'So often people ask me how I compose bhajans! I have no experience of composing music, nor do I hold any special knowledge about it. Whatever bhajans have come through me are His creations. And I feel very blessed to be the channel for His songs. *Parameshwari Jaya Durga*, the very first bhajan, came in a prayerful longing during Navaratri. I wanted to go to the Bangalore ashram since I had heard so much about the pujas which happen there during the Navaratri celebrations. I could not go. Though physically I was in Mumbai [Bombay], my mind was in the ashram. And during one such night, in my sleep, I heard this bhajan. I couldn't wait till the morning. In the middle of the night, I got up and sang it aloud: neither the words nor the tune were mine. It was simply the divine grace pouring over me, and the first bhajan was born. During the Shivratri celebrations ... I silently prayed to Guruji, telling him to send me another bhajan so that I could sing it to him. Within the next few minutes, a new Shiva bhajan was born! And as I started to sing it in [the] satsang, he also started to sing along with me. Everyone looked on in amazement, wondering how he knew the lyrics, when the bhajan was being sung for the first time! For me, he is the embodiment of mother, father, friend, guru ... and much more. He has given me tremendous courage, made me lose my inhibitions, fears, and a whole lot of unnecessary burdens that I was carrying around. And his infinite love, compassion, and patience have made this entire process so smooth and simple!'

Kashi, who holds a Masters in chemical engineering, has become a full-time ashramite and looks after publications and the computer systems. He puts forth his experiences: 'I never knew why, but I had a general feeling that meditation techniques were not for me. Was I not young, intelligent and enthusiastic? And in the midst of all this – meditation? No, this was not for me at all. Yet the day when I went to Khurshed's (my Basic Course teacher) room in his hostel, I saw a photograph of Sri Sri, and instantly felt a deep bond that was beyond explanation, beyond reason, and decided to attend the Basic Course in Khurshed's house. The first day of the Basic Course I felt so much at home; it was like returning, recognizing my family. Of course, it was the Sudarshan Kriya that really blew me off my feet. By the end of the process I felt a sharp shooting pain in my feet as if someone was hammering nails in my soles. I had excruciating pain, and my body arched all the way as if I would be lifted off the floor. Even though I opened my mouth, no sound came out. Unable to bear it any longer, I opened my eyes a little bit, and what did I see – a figure in white, the same enchanting face, the same soothing presence – and everything subsided into a wave of bliss, more ecstasy than I had ever experienced. After the course, for a while, I had to get used to my new bearings. I plunged myself into Art of Living activities, went for satsangs every Thursday, and generally found myself happier than ever before.

'Then the great day came. Gurudev was to pass through Mumbai on the way to Bangalore. A satsang was organized and I found myself helping in the preparation. Soon it was time and the satsang started. While we were eagerly awaiting the arrival of the Guru, Khurshed asked me to go and man the Divine Shop at the entrance of the hall. This meant I couldn't participate in the satsang to my heart's content. I was a trifle dejected, as I felt I wouldn't get to see the Guru. But after the satsang, some of us assembled in Sangeeta Jani's house, where Gurudev was resting for the night. As the night progressed, he sent everyone out and finally only two of us, Harish and myself, were left. At that time, I realized that whatever effort (!) I put into helping would always be rewarded way beyond my imagination.

'Just two months after the Basic Course, I got to know about an Advanced Course in the ashram at Bangalore.

Notwithstanding the fact that it was in the middle of the semester, I just talked to my professors and went to participate in the course. Landing in Bangalore, we hitchhiked to the ashram in a passing vehicle, and finally I was home. The satsang and the silence were awesome. And, on the second day of the Advanced Course, in this perfect setting, Sri Sri walked into the session – majestic, yet subtle, followed by a tumult of emotions, yet serene, an embodiment of silence and love. In the silence I could feel his presence spread as a vast effulgence of grace. And permeating each and every cell of creation, he stood there smiling – it seemed only for me.

'One experience stands out. It was an hour-long meditation and, at the start, Gurudev instructed us to remain perfectly still. I was sitting in the aisle, and after the meditation started, I felt ants crawling all over the body. Dismissing it as an experience in the meditation, I continued to stay still. However, as the meditation proceeded, my whole body was covered [with] red ants, biting me everywhere. However, I still adhered to Gurudev's instruction. Sit still I did, and by the end of the meditation, I had experienced a catharsis beyond description. It was as if he stood by my side helping me through the process. That was when I realized that every experience is just a tool for the Guru to open me up more and more.

'During my first Navaratri at the ashram, I experienced a whole new aspect of my beloved Gurudev. This was the first time I had observed the total silence – a silence that encompassed the surroundings, people, and events. In the midst of the sound of Vedic chanting, the clang of the cymbals and the beat of the drums, Sri Sri sat unmoved, untouched and yet totally immersed in all the happenings.

Without uttering a word, without moving a muscle, he seemed to be doing everything.'

Yet another friend of ours, who prefers to remain anonymous, had this story to tell: 'I was new to the Art of Living and, during an Advanced Course, I had given rather a tart reply to Gurudev – and then immediately regretted it. By the time we all retired for the night, my remorse had reached such intensity that I sat in my room crying bitterly for a couple of hours. I was inconsolable. In the morning, our course leader told us that the previous night Gurudev had been concerned about a woman who had cried in her room for a long time. The course leader went on and explained that Gurudev had asked him to deliver a message to all of us, but especially to the lady who had been crying: "Let go of each moment as it passes. Forgive others, but especially yourself. Let go of all judgements and blame and learn to perceive and honour the Divine who dwells in yourself, as well as in others. The Divine is free of all blame and that is how we all are at the core of our being." I felt such a sweetness in my heart, that not only was Gurudev not offended or angry with me, but [also] that he was concerned about my distress. Later on, I heard Gurudev say, "Remember the guru does not hold faults and weaknesses against you. The guru has come to help you with these faults."'

A fashion designer by profession, Hima Parikh was struggling to maintain a strained marital life till she did the Basic Course: 'Before the Basic Course, I designed clothes – but had never thought that I could design my life. My approach to life was very materialistic and there was no joy in it. I was so lonely. I began to sense that I could not handle my child, my house, my family or my business. At this point my husband suggested that we should separate because our relationship was also deteriorating. But that same month, we took the Basic Course together, and immediately felt a connection in our hearts that had been lacking in the three years of our married life. Thanks to the Sudarshan Kriya, my life changed totally and thanks to this powerful breathing practice my depression and tensions disappeared and for the first time param shanti and param anand (supreme peace and supreme happiness) became more than just words to me. Even before the course was over, I started perceiving the problems and situations in my life in a more positive manner. Soon I went to the Bangalore ashram for the Advanced Course, but it was really just an excuse to meet Gurudev. The ashram felt like home. Every moment spent with Gurudev was filled with joy, knowledge, and love. His playfulness provokes laughter but, even in his mischief, there is profound wisdom.'

The list of such stories is endless.

Chapter Ten

The Miracles

In science knowledge comes first and then faith follows. In spirituality faith comes first and then knowledge follows.

Westerners are particularly wary of 'miracles', although Christ is supposed to have performed many. I am uneasy, for instance, when I read about the life of Puttaparthi Sai Baba and hear of him appearing in three different places at the same time when he was young. (Puttaparthi is situated in the Anantpur district of Andhra Pradesh.) Yet, the one time I met Sai Baba, I definitely felt 'something' as I witnessed him materialize vibhuti (holy ash). I have also talked to some of his disciples – intelligent, coherent, and serious men and women – who told me they had seen him with their own eyes changing a stone into a diamond, or silver into gold. So I give gurus the benefit of the doubt that they must be capable of performing miracles, although the Cartesian streak in me still has qualms about it. For me the greatest of miracles that a guru can perform is to change his disciples' natures, a near-impossible task. Nevertheless, a book about Sri Sri cannot skip the subject of miracles, as it is the most common refrain of his disciples: 'Guruji performed this miracle or that miracle on me'; 'I couldn't walk, I walked'; 'I had cancer, I got cured'; and 'I was blind, I saw.' We have now met so many good, serious, and truthful teachers and disciples of AOL, who have told us about the miracles which happened to them. Having observed Sri Sri for about seven years now, for me the greatest of miracles is the smile and energy that manifest themselves in people through his presence.

On the final day of one of the Advanced Courses we attended, a number of people came on stage in the experience-sharing session to recount what they had witnessed or gone through.

Shyam Sunder Sardana, an industrialist from Haryana, reported a remarkable recovery from a near-fatal heart condition. 'I had been a heart patient since my forties. With my angina I had to take precautions due to high blood pressure and hypertension. I had a heart attack at forty-eight, and had been on heavy medication since. I had my first heart surgery at 56 when I was diagnosed as having blocked arteries. In February of 1998, when I had aggravated breathing problems, I went for a detailed check-up. Tests showed that I was just on the brink of death. All the physicians gave me a maximum of six months to live. I was advised not to climb stairs, nor to leave the room. I would feel breathlessness and could hardly walk 1500 yards.

'In May of 1999 during this bedridden condition, I read about the Basic Course in the Sunday news magazine, and on Monday I contacted the Art of Living teacher, Nityanand. I told him of my problem, and took the Basic Course the next week. After the course, there was a sea change in my condition. I could move about and my health improved considerably. In July, I went to the doctor to see if I could travel to Rishikesh to take an Advanced Course. When I was examined, the doctor was astonished. He exclaimed: "Is this the same heart I examined last month?" And I told him: "Yes, but there's a little change. I have switched over to Sudarshan Kriya in addition to the pills from you!" He had a good laugh.

By the time I met Gurudev and did the Advanced Course, I was fully back in shape. Up till now I have had no problems. I have travelled to Germany and walked up snow-clad mountain slopes. I, who was given just six months to live, and that too as a vegetable in bed, am now hale and hearty and have lived a normal life for the last three years, by the grace of the Guru.'

Namrita's roommate, Dr Ramola Prabhu, had a different story to share. 'The phone [in our house in New York] rang at four in the morning.... It was a nurse from the Shock Trauma Unit in Maryland. Our son [Gokul] had just had surgery for a deep laceration in his right temple. We stood trembling and unbelieving as the chief nurse reassured us that we were very lucky parents and could now take our son back home. My husband, Ganesh, and our two daughters rushed to Maryland, while I stayed behind in New York. The same afternoon that Gokul returned home from the hospital, Gurudev arrived in New York. Amazingly, the people who were supposed to pick him up arrived much later and I found myself alone with him at the airport, just as the heart had desired. While I was still groping for words to tell him, before I could utter anything, I heard him say, "Gokul had an accident, didn't he? Don't worry, he will be okay." Unashamedly, I let the tears of gratitude flow unabated! What Gokul related to me, when I got back home, was nothing short of a miracle. It was dark and, trying to avoid another car driving towards him in the wrong lane, he hit a lamppost. His right side was soaked in blood and every time he tried to stand up, he fainted. Out of nowhere, a "man" appeared from the darkness and asked Gokul if he needed help. No car, no light, no other sound, just this man offering to help. Soon the police arrived and Gokul was flown by helicopter to the Shock Trauma Unit. I called the police station the next day, wanting to thank the person who had brought help and saved my son. The answer I got was amazing – "There is no record of anyone calling." Who was this man in the darkness who helped Gokul?'

Snjezana Nisevic, an AOL teacher from Croatia, recounted the story of Nexhmedin: 'We started to spread Guruji's knowledge in Kosovo immediately after the war. It was hard and wonderful work and one would often have to stick AOL posters on tanks. Kosovo is inhabited by orthodox Muslims who are closed to new knowledge, and at the same time are wonderful, hospitable, and full of gratitude and respect for this knowledge, as soon as they open up. Nexhmedin, for instance, is a twenty-six-year-old man from Kosovo. He is married and has a small son. The beginning of all the wars in Balkan found him in the Serbian army fighting against the Croats. From that army, he ran away to Bosnia where he joined the Muslim army. There he went through the worst moments of his life, lying in a mass grave among dead bodies. From there, he ran away to Kosovo and joined the Kosovo army in war against the Serbian army. When the war ended, Nexhmedin wandered in the mountains on the border with Albania completely lost and unable to return to his family and resume normal life. He was wounded in his spine and unable to walk without crutches. However, the most serious consequence he suffered was a heavy form of PTSD (post-traumatic stress disorder), manifested as epileptic attacks several times per day, long periods of amnesia, and loss of consciousness. When he finally returned home, his family was desperate because of his condition.

'We persuaded him to do the AOL Basic Course. During the course, Nexhmedin felt so much better that he travelled to another city with [the] teachers and went through the Basic Course once again. After the course, all the PTSD symptoms disappeared! There were no more epileptic attacks, amnesia or loss of consciousness! And all this in a period of two weeks! After one month, Nexhmedin came to learn Sahaj Samadhi meditation. With a smile on his face, he said that he had been doing the programme regularly and that he did not need crutches any longer. Now he has a great desire to meet Guruji.'

After some prodding, Vasanthi Narayanan, our Advanced Course teacher, told us her miraculous story: 'I came in contact with Guruji around 1988. At the time I was suffering from numerous health problems, spinal problems, and spondylitis with a lot of breathing difficulties. The doctors had given me only six months to live as all these were putting pressure on my heart. I was in a depressed state of mind and the family also reflected this as they were worried about me. I used to pray to Krishna every day. One day, I sat and prayed that he take me today – I didn't even want to live the six months given to me. While I was praying, I had a vision. It was as if it had rained and I saw a ten-year-old boy, dressed in white like Krishna, stretching out his hand to me. I was down in a deep dark well and he asked me to take his hand to come up. As I tried to hold his hand, he just picked me up in his arms and brought me up. That energy and that light gave a wonderful warmth inside me and I thought God had taken me already. After an hour or two I opened my eyes and realized that I was still in this world.

'Within two days of this experience there was a satsang in the house of somebody working in the Indian High Commission in Singapore to which I was invited. When I got there it was as if they were waiting for someone, some yogi. I did not want to talk to anybody. The door opened and suddenly Gurudev came in and I felt: "How come? Yesterday you were within me and today you are here." I felt this emptiness in me. I did not have any other thought other than "Here is my Krishna." I decided to do the Basic Course which was very painful and difficult, but after some time I felt very good and perceived that the whole body had changed. I removed my lumbar belt, my collar and I could BREATHE. Soon after that I came to the ashram, in Bangalore, and stayed for 19 days. With Guruji's grace I was completely cured during this time and I went back a new person, with renewed energy. I was fulfilled. It was not the old Vasanthi, on the mental or any other level. This was a real miracle for me. Before coming in contact with Gurudev, I was a very reserved person and would not meet many people. Now I travel all over the world to teach courses. And it is quite amazing how I meet people and feel at home everywhere. I feel guided wherever I go and know I am taken care of.'

It was then the turn of Eva Lewarne, an American who is no novice to spiritual life, having been a student of a Tibetan Buddhist lama for nine years, to come on the stage and describe her experiences: 'I first met him when I went to attend a public talk given by him in Toronto. Although I was reluctant to go, once there, I experienced one of the most profound moments of my life! As soon as I sat down in the auditorium, I felt bathed in an atmosphere of joy, peace, and incredible love, which intensified when he walked in and all I could do was sit in meditative bliss. The room seemed to fill with the most amazing perfume and there was such a profound feeling, which I shared with my friend, that here was a man at whose feet I could sit for the rest of my life. I felt totally relaxed, despite the fact that I had recently been diagnosed with cancer of the ovaries at Princess Margaret Hospital [in Toronto] and the doctor felt the need for a quick date for the operation, as soon as he got the result of a particular blood test. But right now, I was totally oblivious to everything else and loved the way Guruji spontaneously answered the numerous questions put to him. I felt reluctant to leave, and hung around in the hope that he might walk by me. To my amazement he did, and the thought flashed through my mind that if I touched him, I would be healed. I touched him. And, to cut a long story short, I went back to the hospital the following Tuesday and heard from my doctor that I was a very baffling case – my blood test came back negative! Saying thank you seems very insignificant in the face of the miracle Guruji performed on me.'

Our friend Raghu Raj Raja, whom Gurudev once sent to Japan to conduct Art of Living courses, recounted this story: 'A twenty-three-year-old girl named Yako, who had [had] an accident when she was 16, was brought to one of the courses. She was in a wheelchair, unable to walk or even lift her hands. Yako and her mother had come with tremendous hope. They were tired of all the medications that had been prescribed over the years. Though I doubted whether she could handle the course, I allowed Yako to sit through the first day of instruction. That night, Gurudev telephoned me from Germany, and even before I could begin, he said: "Doesn't matter even if the pranayama positions are not all right, she can still do the Kriya." After the first Sudarshan Kriya, Yako found that she could lift her hands and bring them down at will. After the second Kriya, she could actually walk, with a bit of help. The girl and her mother were overwhelmed. Tears of gratitude flowed from their eyes, and they wished to take the first opportunity to meet Gurudev. Yako's experience was aired on Tokyo Radio, which inspired numerous people to join the Art of Living.'

Dr Saran, a paediatrician from Mongolia, who has travelled around the world with her husband who is a top official with WHO, had this to say: 'When Guruji was in Ulan Bator, on a state visit ... we were amazed at the devotion and connectedness of the Mongolian people, most of whom were seeing him for the first time. Heads bowed and eyes filled with tears, they came in hundreds to have a glimpse of the "Living God" as they called him. In the crowd was a lady who had been paralysed and bedridden for years. When she saw Guruji's photo in the newspaper, she immediately recognized him as her guru, rose from her bed, and walked to the satsang for his darshan, where she shared her healing experience, as we looked on in wonder.'

Sangeeta Jani (whom we have met in Chapter 6) still remembers the day when her apartment caught fire: 'Usually at around 7.00 p.m. I take a shower and meditate but, on this particular day, a friend of mine coaxed me to go out with her. While I was out, I felt very restless. On reaching home, I found the whole building in darkness and water all around. My neighbours rushed to tell me that my entire floor had caught fire and everything had been destroyed. For a couple of minutes, I couldn't register what they were saying. When I went upstairs, I was shocked to see the state of my apartment. Everything seemed to be destroyed. Then, through the shambles, I saw my altar still covered with silk, adorned by Gurudev's padukas [sandals]. A short circuit had occurred and all that remained were the altar and my Art of Living papers. Not even a toothbrush had been spared; even an audiocassette lying on top of a satsang book got burnt, but the book survived not only the fire, but also the water from the fire brigade rescue team. If I had taken my shower according to routine, I would have been trapped. With the Guru's grace, deliverance came in the form of my friend!'

Dr Ramola Prabhu shared with us another inspiring healing experience: 'A few years ago my aunt was diagnosed with an undifferentiated, very malignant metastatic tumour in the neck. The doctors did not know where the primary site was, and so my aunt suffered the ravages of full-body radiation and chemotherapy. She was given less than six months to live, and decided with her husband to spend some time with their grandchildren in Europe, as their son was settled there. We convinced them to visit us in the US. Their itinerary changed and they arrived in Baltimore. Coincidentally, the same weekend a Basic Course was happening in our home. Throughout the Sudarshan Kriya, my aunt complained of a severe burning sensation in her neck, but somehow she completed the course. Shortly thereafter they returned to India. It is now almost seven years since my aunt was told she had six months to live. She regularly practises the Kriya, is very much alive and completely healthy. Currently she runs a school for the underprivileged children of her area.'

M, an English lady, concluded the session by recollecting her experiences: 'Two years ago, I needed surgery to remove my uterus. The doctor was not competent enough and botched it. He damaged the wall of my bladder and that affected my kidney. After the surgery my abdominal pain remained, and in the next three months it worsened. I decided to come to

India for better medical treatment. A scan showed a foreign body lodged in my abdomen, a small clip left behind by the surgeon in the previous operation! The doctors here decided to perform another surgery to remove the object. I decided to wait till Guruji's return from Germany and have his darshan before going ahead with the operation. As the pain grew worse, and based on the doctors' prognosis, I resigned myself to the surgery. I spoke to Gurudev over the telephone and he asked me to do ... meditation. On the seventh morning I had to go for a pre-operative scan. The next morning, Guruji arrived and I went for a puja at the ashram before going to collect the report. When I reached the medical centre, I found the doctors were incredulous; there was no trace of the object. The clip had completely disappeared!'

The experiences I had heard about were truly breath-taking for me, and I decided to ask Sri Sri about them, during our next meeting: 'What do you think about all these healing experiences and miracles?' He smiled and answered: 'Life is a mystery. It has to be lived, not understood.' I left his cottage, not entirely clear what he meant, yet beginning to ponder over the answer.

I went back to my room, which I shared with S. B. Ganguly, an industrialist from Calcutta. He also had his own story to tell! Early one morning, when he went for a walk from his house in an upmarket locality of the city, he was kidnapped and taken to a remote place. The kidnappers were hardened criminals, and they demanded a fat ransom. The news made headlines. Kept in a dark room for many days, he prayed intensely to Guruji during that period. Throughout the nightmare, Ganguly distinctly heard Guruji's voice assuring him, 'I am with you and nothing will happen to you.' After some time, suddenly Ganguly noticed a drastic change in the attitude of the criminals, who started taking care of him, feeding him, and even providing him with his daily diabetic pills! Soon, without making any demands, they released Ganguly, with a note of apology for the inconvenience!!

As Ganguly finished the story, Sanjeev who was quietly observing us talking, showed me a letter from Cathy Champion in St Louis (in Missouri, USA), reporting a curious incident that occurred to her husband, which was reproduced in Sri Sri's book *An Intimate Note to the Sincere Seeker*. When Cathy's husband Mike, a fitness freak who never missed work, suddenly complained about pain in his shoulder, she knew it was something serious. The MRI showed damage to nerves and muscles; the diagnosis after studying the X-rays was a torn rotator cuff, and surgery was scheduled. When Cathy received a flier for a talk by Sri Sri scheduled the day before the surgery, she and Mike thought it was a good way to spend the evening. During the course of the talk, Cathy found Sri Sri's voice and his persona strangely familiar. At the end of the talk, they decided to stand in a 300-people-long queue to meet Sri Sri, which was quite unusual for them. When their turn came, Cathy found herself asking for Mike's safety during next day's surgery. Sri Sri called for a rose and handed it to Mike, advising him to keep the flower by his side, and assuring him that 'all will be well'. And so it was.

Finally, Rajshree shared her amazing experiences: The very day she landed at Bangalore from Gujarat, Sri Sri asked her to go to Bombay, adding: 'You will have a blast!' Reluctantly, Rajshree went there, and organized a course in Chembur, a suburb situated quite a distance away from where she was staying. On the second day of the course (12 March 1993), the infamous Bombay bomb blasts took place, killing over

200 persons and causing tremendous damage to property. Large-scale riots ensued. The areas that Rajshree had to cross to reach the course venue were among the most sensitive and riot-prone. Also, there was a limited curfew in effect. Determined to keep her commitment to the course, Rajshree persuaded a taxi driver to take her to Chembur, and miraculously, the taxi deposited her at the venue safely, amidst looting, arson, and looting! After returning from the course, Rajshree found the phone ringing. It was Sri Sri who said jokingly: 'I told you, you would have a blast!'

Sri Sri was scheduled to transit through Bombay the next day from Germany, and Rajshree tried to persuade him to take a flight via Delhi or Chennai for security reasons. He refused and gave her the flight details, but Rajshree was unsure if she would be able to make it to the airport due to the curfew. On the next day of the course, all 60 participants were in attendance as it was a gated colony. One of the participants asked her permission to leave the course early, which she refused. At the end of that session, a lady invited her for tea at her home. As Rajshree was walking towards her destination, she noticed the gentleman, who had sought her permission to leave the course early, entering a house marked 'Commissioner of Police'. Rajshree remarked that it was a good tactic to keep the intruders away! The lady laughed, saying that the man was indeed the commissioner of police, and that he had sought permission to leave the course early due to the curfew! When Rajshree told her that she had to leave for the airport to receive Guruji, the commissioner volunteered to drop her, saying that it would be impossible for her to reach otherwise, as 'shoot-at-sight' orders had been imposed in the area. Just as both of them reached the airport in the commissioner's car, Sri Sri arrived at the airport gate, and remarked: 'See, I told you, you would find a way!'

The more I think about all these experiences, the more Sri Sri's words echo in my mind: 'Life is a mystery. It has to be lived, not understood.'

Chapter Eleven

The Search for Scientific Proof

Life without wisdom is incomplete,
Wisdom that does not give rise to feelings
 is incomplete,
Feeling that does not transfer into action
 is incomplete,
Action that does not give rise to fulfilment
 is incomplete,
Fulfilment is returning to self.

I have now been with the Art of Living long enough to recognize the authenticity of the claims of healing experiences made by people around me. After all, my own breathing disorders healed dramatically after the practice of the Sudarshan Kriya. Yet, my mind, groomed by Western upbringing, needed additional scientific proof. For some time, I wondered why scientific establishments did not take up the active lead in measuring the impact of these practices. The question remained with me, until I received an invitation to attend the 'Science of Breath' symposium from the All India Institute of Medical Sciences (AIIMS), New Delhi. I happened to be in the capital at that time, and attended the symposium a couple of times. I could sense that the results were dramatic, although I could not understand the medical jargon. This is my understanding of what science has proved. Basically, there have been four major findings on the impact of the Sudarshan Kriya and related breathing practices taught in the Art of Living course.

AIIMS has taken EEG pictures of the brain. The change in colour indicates 'high beta wave activity', which means greater integration of the left (logical) and right (aesthetic) hemispheres of the brain, and improved awareness. This shows that the person's mind is in a state of 'relaxed wakefulness' and 'heightened awareness'.

Dr Geeta of Bangalore University presented a paper on the capability of the Sudarshan Kriya to treat depression – 70 per cent of the people who practised this Kriya overcame depression. The practice was as effective as popular drugs, without the dependence or side-effects.

Studies have also shown that the Sudarshan Kriya is an effective stress-buster. Proxies of stress such as the stress hormone (serum cortisol) and the stress enzyme (serum lactose) show a marked decrease after the practice, indicating a relaxation response. Doctors surmise that the glucose spared from the muscles and red blood cells (RBCs) during the practice are made available to the brain, leading to a state of body relaxation and mental alertness. This study also showed that levels of the serum cortisol in Art of Living teachers were dramatically low, probably due to the regularity of practice and the impact of the advanced programmes.

Of some interest to the medical community vis-à-vis the Sudarshan Kriya is also the dramatic increase in natural cells in cancer patients (such cells kill the cancer cells) and the rise in good cholesterol simultaneously with a reduction in bad cholesterol in the system. Are these metabolic changes the reason why Sudarshan Kriya is able to heal a wide array of diseases? When I posed this question to Dr Manikantan, the Ayurvedic teacher at the Bangalore ashram, he replied: 'When the balance of the doshas (elements that go into making a body type) is restored in the system, diseases are automatically cured.' Sri Sri has remarked on different occasions about the need to attend to health. 'Half the health we spend gaining our wealth,' he says, 'and then spend half our wealth trying to gain back our health – this is not a very intelligent thing to do.'

Medical Courses

AOL courses are not only psychological tools for feeling better and for leading a more harmonious life, but also they are extremely efficient in treating psychiatric, psychological, and medical problems, which have often left modern medicine baffled. Depression, for instance, is a disabling condition that takes the joy out of life for millions around the world – men, women, and children – regardless of race, income, or family background. Depression also contributes, remarks Sri Sri, 'to the downward spiral of many diseases, from cancer and HIV to asthma and cardiovascular diseases. Finding an effective treatment for depression is a global health concern.' The Art of Living Course for Depression offers a variety of techniques that have been documented by independent medical studies to be effective in alleviating this condition. These simple yet powerful techniques have definite advantages over many other forms of treatment because they are free from negative side-effects, cut healthcare costs, and are easy to learn and practise in daily life.

However, due to the often long-term and chronic nature of depression, Art of Living Courses for Depression usually run longer than the regular Art of Living courses and are sometimes taught as in-residence programmes.

Many of us, as we age, incur the risk of coronary heart disease (CHD). In fact, anyone can develop CHD regardless of age, sex, race or ethnic background. Sometimes, there may be no warning signs and symptoms, and even if there are any, either they are not noticed or they are ignored. The history of CHD is higher in the urban population than in the rural, and is a major cause for premature death. When three risk factors like hyperlipidaemia (high fat and cholesterol content in blood), hypertension, and smoking together afflict an individual, the chances of a heart attack are seven times higher, whereas the risk is twofold when these are individually present. Whatever the risk factor, the basic pathology of CHD is deposition of LDL cholesterol (harmful cholesterol), fat, and other substances on the walls of the coronary arteries. These deposits thicken the arterial walls and narrow the arteries, which slows or blocks the flow of blood. The heart receives a constant supply of oxygen through blood; any blockage of the flow may result in chest pain (angina pectoris) and myocardial infarction (heart attack) or even death.

It is my experience, as an ex-smoker and a sportsman, that regular Sudarshan Kriya practice, apart form Ujjai, Pranayama, and Bhastrika (these three are different types of breathing exercises) can work wonders: one attains better all-round health, more stamina, and more lung capacity. Also, the eyesight improves. My humble findings seem to have a medical sanction: the All India Institute of Medical Sciences conducted a study on 46 normal participants, whose lipid profiles – which involves the study of serum cholestrol (total), HDL cholesterol (good cholesterol), LDL cholesterol (harmful cholesterol) and triglycerides – were analysed before the start of the Sudarshan Kriya practice and subsequently on the seventh and forty-fifth day after regular Sudarshan Kriya practice. Amazingly, there was a significant decrease in serum total cholesterol, LDL cholesterol, and lipid peroxidation, and an increase in HDL cholesterol. The hypocholestrimic action of Sudarshan Kriya practice suggests that it can be used as a tool for the prevention of a deranged lipid profile and hypertension, which is a major risk factor for CHD. Which, put in plain language, means that if you practise Sudarshan Kriya, the chances of your suffering a heart attack after the age of 50 are five times lesser.

One morning Namrita and I were sipping our tea on the veranda, when our maidservant Radha, arrived weeping, totally shattered as a result of her husband Raju's habit of heavy drinking. He had come home totally drunk the night before, beat her up, slapped the children, and then collapsed in a drunken stupor. Seeing her pain and anguish, we went and met a sorrowful Raju a little later. We reached out to him, talked to him and convinced him to do the Art of Living course for alcoholics.

All of us have felt, at one time or the other, the urge to indulge in mood-elevating experiences, such as alcohol, grass, or even stronger hallucinogenic stuff. Alcohol seems to be, not only in the West, but also unfortunately in India, the one socially accepted custom. But sadly, the repeated consumption of alcoholic beverages ultimately leads to a dreadful dependence on them, wherein one needs to drink more and more to get the same pleasurable experience. And anyone who has tried to break the habit must have gone through very unpleasant withdrawal symptoms. Alcoholism is a dreadful disease which is creating havoc in the world. It not only virtually empties people's wallets, but also adversely affects their mind and their health. Here are a few statistics to prove my point: In 1976, liquor manufacturers in India utilized 169.4 million litres of absolute alcohol, enough to manufacture 350 million bottles of rum. The figure rose to 207.9 million litres in 1981, 331 million litres in 1985, 459 million litres in 1991, and 700 million litres in 2001.

This high proportion of problem-drinkers in India has led
to more frequent visits to hospitals and clinics due to alcohol-
related illnesses. The studies done at a large general hospital
in Bangalore revealed that 40 per cent of all males and 6.6
per cent of all females admitted for medical and surgical
problems had a drinking problem. Many treatment approaches
have been used to treat alcoholism all over the world, such
as pharmacological therapy, disulfiram therapy, aversion
therapy, and non-pharmacological therapy (for example,
alcoholics anonymous, psychotherapy, relapse therapy). While
each of these approaches has met with limited success in
achieving abstinence, the pharmacological treatment appears
to be the most promising in the management of alcoholism.
But still, the rate of relapse is in the range of 40 to 50 per
cent. This is where Sri Sri's all-round Sudarshan Kriya comes
in; it was tested in 1999 in NIMHANS (National Institute
of Mental Health and Neurosciences) of Bangalore on 60
heavily alcohol-dependent men, who were willing to stay
closeted for 30 days. The patients were first detoxified for
seven days, and then randomly divided into two treatment
groups of 30 patients each. Group 1 members received only
the standard treatment: family therapy, psychotherapy, with
diazepam prescribed for up to six months after the group
session. Group 2 members were made to go into a state of
silence and practise yogasanas, pranayama, and Sudarshan
Kriya under supervision. After twenty-five days, all those
practising Sudarshan Kriya showed marked improvement
physically and psychologically and are today living without
relapse, while 75 per cent of Group 1 relapsed within six
months. Raju was one of the lucky ones and has stayed clean
for many years. Radha's smile says it all.

One of the most dreaded diseases of modern times is of course cancer, which has touched all of us in some manner: a mother, a father, a cherished uncle, or a brother maybe, slowly wasting away before our horrified eyes. The confirmed diagnosis of cancer leads to a challenging and stressful situation in anyone's life. And even though cancer is more survivable than ever before, coping with cancer can take a heavy physical, mental, and emotional toll. Mounting scientific data suggest that the immune system function, the quality, and even the very length of life, are all profoundly impacted by one's mental and emotional state. Healing and resistance to disease are not simply functions of the body – one's state of mind and emotions also significantly affect one's physical health. Whether you are dealing with the side-effects of cancer treatment or the emotional upheaval of a recent cancer diagnosis, Art of Living Cancer Courses offer a wealth of practical techniques and knowledge that promote health at every level. They feature the Sudarshan Kriya technique, which supports the healing process by reducing the effects of stress, by restoring vital energy, and by enabling one to sleep more peacefully at night. It also plays a vital role in the effective interaction among the mind, the body, and the emotions to create overall well-being.

Not only do we live in a world full of stress, but also many of us encounter traumatic situations – brought about by wars, natural calamities, diseases, rapes, and road accidents – that leave behind terrible after-effects. Helping such trauma victims regain their equilibrium through the different pranayama techniques has proved very beneficial. As already mentioned, AOL volunteers have worked with those uprooted by the 26 January 2001 earthquake that hit Gujarat and in the war-torn Balkans.

A study of the effectiveness of the Sudarshan Kriya and the other breathing exercises on trauma survivors has also been conducted at NIMHANS, India's premier institute for the study of neuroscience and mental health. It has been found (see Appendix 2) that the levels of cortisol decreased significantly within 21 days in subjects who practised Sudarshan Kriya. NIMHANS research has also documented accelerated neuronal processing of, and recovery from, stressful stimuli. This means the brain returns to normal more quickly after receiving stressful stimuli.

Additionally, sleep disturbances measured in depressed populations normalized, improving both the length and the quality of sleep.

Another pilot study on persons affected by trauma, conducted by the Republic of Slovenia's Institute for Rehabilitation, documented significant reductions in anxiety levels (as measured by the widely used State-Trait Anxiety Inventory or STAI) within five days of learning Sudarshan Kriya and significant increases in alpha activity and in plasma prolactin, which are believed to produce feelings of well-being. It was also found that the Kriya induced high-frequency EEG activity, which is indicative of greater concentration and mental focus.

Ayurveda

Sri Sri Ravi Shankar is a champion of the renaissance of Ayurveda, because he feels that many of today's so-called incurable diseases can be treated by this form of medication. Ayurveda has been tried and tested thoroughly over the centuries, and can be used very effectively to treat all kinds of disorders. What is Ayurveda? It is the science of restoring balance in an individual on a physical, psychological, and spiritual level: Ayur (of life)-veda (science) uses herbs, diet, lifestyle, yoga, vedic astrology, colour therapy, energy points (using pressure, puncture, heat, and oils), aromatherapy, gemstones, vastu shastra (similar to Feng Shui), and various other therapeutic means to promote well-being – sukham.

'The unique constitutions of our body/mind/sense complexes with which we are born move out of balance by inappropriate diet and lifestyles, as well as unresolved emotions,' points out Sri Sri Ravi Shankar. 'These imbalances eventually progress into disease. Ayurvedic medicine recognizes and treats a traditional seven-stage pathogenesis, only the last two obvious stages of which, disease and deformity, are usually diagnosed and treated in Western medicine.'

As in medical traditions from Persia to China, and elsewhere, 'pulse diagnosis' is used in Ayurvedic medicine as a principal diagnostic tool to ascertain a person's present and past physical and mental health. By understanding and applying what it means to actively live in harmony with universal laws that influence our existence, Ayurveda guides us in healing, preventing disorders, rejuvenating, and revitalizing ourselves on the physical, psychological, and spiritual levels.

According to Ayurveda, every individual has a unique combination of physical, mental, and emotional characteristics. The body, the mind, and consciousness work together in maintaining balance. Internal and external factors can act to disturb one's balance, and both physical and mental disturbances are reflected through the skin. Also, the Ayurvedic system recognizes that both the environment and human beings are composed of five basic elements: air, space, fire, water, and earth. The predominance of these elements affects the three metabolic characteristics of individuals, referred to as doshas. These three doshas are vata, pitta, and kapha, and individuals can be classified as belonging to one of these three constitutions or as a combination of two or even three of the doshas.

The goal of Ayurvedic Healthcare Products and Services is to help individuals take advantage of the strengths of their doshas, while, at the same time, limiting the weaknesses. This is made possible by maintaining the doshas at an optimal level through a range of treatments collated in Ayurvedic texts.

The Art of Living Foundation has a dispensary that manufactures a growing variety of Ayurvedic products, which are meant to maintain and/or enhance general health, prevent imbalance, cleanse tissues, and purge toxins. They do not claim to cure any doctor-defined disease. In no case do AOL doctors recommend or prescribe herbs, nor do they diagnose, treat, prevent or cure disease. On the contrary, they will advise you to always consult a qualified physician for any medical condition.

Here are a few sample medicines: Makardhwaj, is a general tonic and a traditional Ayurvedic male aphrodisiac. Shatavari (*Asparagus racemosus*) is the main rejuvenating herb for the female, as Ashwagandha is for the male. Shatavari nourishes and cleanses the blood and the female reproductive organs. It is particularly useful for women who are nursing as well as for those affected by menopause, besides those who have undergone a hysterectomy. Shilajit (*Asphaltum*) is a general rejuvenator that promotes strength and immunity and is also used to support the proper functioning of the urinary tract and the prostate. It also reduces excess kapha. Triphla detoxifies and rejuvenates. This formulation is based on a tridoshic Ayurvedic formula. It is used as a mild laxative and can be taken both for preventive and curative purposes. It strengthens the digestion and improves eye vision and is beneficial for liver problems and hair loss as well. It is also used for weight management and for improving the complexion. Triphla Guggul minimizes the accumulation of toxins in the gastrointestinal tract and joints, and supports proper digestion and elimination of waste products. It decongests the body channels, removes toxins from the tissues, rekindles the digestive juices, and promotes healthy metabolism. It also removes excess kapha from the body.

In India virtually every third shop is an allopathic pharmacy selling drugs made by multinationals, which sometimes do more harm than good. Antibiotics, for instance, kill not only the disease-causing microbes but also some good elements in our body, whereas neem (*Azadirachta indica*) only destroys the harmful components (neem is shakti says Guruji). It is high time that India rediscovered the wonder that is Ayurveda, the oldest medical system of the world still in practice.

Chapter Twelve

Sri Sri's Answers for the World Today

The self knows neither sorrow nor death, yet in it flow all relative events. It is easy to be detached when you are not in love. Being in utter love and yet undisturbed, caring yet not worried, persistent yet not perturbed — all are the obvious signs of self shining through.

Over the last few years of association with Sri Sri, I have come to notice how his model of social reform contains many answers that the world is searching for today. Perhaps that is why increasingly Sri Sri and other teachers are invited to talk on a range of topics in many diverse forums. I have found many of Sri Sri's perspectives to be of immense value in understanding and addressing the core of the twenty-first century issues, which includes terrorism, religion, and education. Here are my compilations of some of Sri Sri's question-and-answer sessions.

Terrorism

I heard from John Osborne (whom we have come across in Chapter 6) about a curious encounter that Sri Sri had with a fanatic, at a public talk in Washington D.C. A tall, well-built man who was sitting at the back of the hall suddenly walked onto the stage, yelling and gesticulating at Sri Sri. As he approached within striking distance, raising his hands as if to strangle Sri Sri, the 300-strong audience sat frozen with shock. As he looked into Sri Sri's eyes, Guruji just raised his hand, and said: 'Wait.' No one knows exactly what happened immediately after that. Anyway, the attacker sat where he was, with tears in his eyes. Someone from the audience took the attacker aside, and Sri Sri continued the discourse, saying: 'It is the ignorance in us that makes us small minded. Fanaticism and rigidity will keep you far away from Divinity. Those who profess fanaticism do not need condemnation but compassion.'

Terrorism induces fear and increases poverty, suffering, and loss of life with no apparent gain to anyone. Instead of offering or seeking solutions, terrorism looks to destruction as an answer. In acts of terrorism, human values are lost.

Why do people turn to terrorism?

The first factor is frustration accompanied by desperation to achieve a goal. When people are desperate to achieve some goal and are unable to do it, the desperation engenders violence in them.

The second factor is belief in a non-verifiable concept of merit that could lead one to heaven: 'If I die fighting for God, then I will go to heaven, because God wants this act to happen.' Who knows? No one can verify these statements.

The third is a staunch belief that 'my way is the only way'.

The fourth is ignoring human values in order to achieve a goal.

And the fifth is the lack of respect or honour for life itself.

Terrorism is thus based on a concept of God as favouring some and being angry with others. This notion undermines the omnipresence and omnipotence of God. How can an omnipresent God exclude some people? How can an omnipotent God be angry? Anger and frustration arise when someone is unable to do something or control something. With this limited idea of God, you become the saviour of

God rather than the servant of God. God is a poor fellow sitting somewhere getting angry, and you are going to help him.

Terrorism fails to recognize that God loves variety and diversity; that many different schools of thought exist in this world. It does not respect or honour life. Terrorism arises when someone identifies himself first and foremost as a member of a particular religion, and then is ready to give up his life for that limited identity. We need first to identify ourselves as part of the Divine and, after that, as human beings.

Q: What is the remedy for terrorism?
Sri Sri: As long as there is limited understanding [with] limited wisdom being imparted in fundamentalist and fanatical schools, there is no way we can rid this world of terrorism.

We have to broaden our vision and educate people about all the different religions and cultural traditions of the world. Religious and spiritual leaders, in particular, should have a broad understanding of cultures and religions. Every mullah, every priest, and rabbi should know something about all other religions. If we learn to broaden our vision and deepen our roots, people will not fall into a narrow idea of the will of God; they will see life in a broad perspective. It's not just religion that makes people become terrorists; there can be social and political reasons also.

Next, we have to educate people in the human values of friendliness, compassion, cooperation, a sense of belonging, and spirituality. We can say that spirituality is that which nourishes the human values of compassion, love, caring, sharing, and acceptance. Spirituality is finding a way to calm the mind and go deep in your prayers, irrespective of what prayer you do or what religion you follow. It is honouring the values that are found in all religions. And it is concern for the common good of one and all, accommodating diversity of thought, deed, and behaviour in the world.

We have to learn how to cope with the stress of life. Stress and tension are the root cause of violence. Have a sense of belonging to this planet and all its people. Cultivate confidence in achieving a noble goal in a peaceful, non-violent manner. This confidence comes from your inner strength. There are many examples for us of people who have done this: Martin Luther King in the North American continent, Nelson Mandela in the African continent, Mahatma Gandhi in the Asian continent. Only spiritual upliftment can weed out the destructive tendency in the human mind.

Q: Where was God on September 11?
Sri Sri: Where was God when the Columbine killings occurred? Where was God when the Mississippi River flooded? Where was God when there was a tornado in Florida or the earthquake in Gujarat? Why are you asking only about September 11? Three hundred and sixty-five days a year calamitous events happen in the world. Whether man-made or natural, calamity is part of life on this planet. We cannot question the existence of Divinity over an event, pleasant or unpleasant. A faith based on God preventing calamities will be weak. Faith is that which stands the test of events. Many of the Christian saints and apostles were persecuted or executed. If they had questioned, 'Where is God? Where is God?' faith would have had no place in their lives. Faith is something much bigger, much more fundamental to life than the events that happen throughout life. God is not a toy for your security or a concept

for your convenience. God is love. God is the substratum of this universe, the basis of this existence. God is the space in which all things happen.

Q: In the face of such evil, isn't it hard not to question whether there is a God?
Sri Sri: If you have to question whether something is there or not, you must have a concept about it. And if events shake that concept, then the concept will have to change. If you know that God is love and you see that there is love in the world, then you won't question God. But if you think God exists for your security, then when you are in trouble, when you have problems, this question will certainly arise in your mind. And when you have a limited understanding of your life, not knowing that the life energy in you is eternal, is indestructible, is a continuum, then, too, you may question whether there is a God or not. See that God is all-pervading consciousness, that that alone exists, that nothing else exists. You never question whether atoms exist or not; you know atoms exist. That which is the basis of an atom, that field, that space in which everything exists, everything blossoms, grows and perishes, that basic substratum of this creation – let that be your understanding of God. Then you won't ever ask if God exists.

Q: What attitude should we have towards terrorists?
Sri Sri: We need to be compassionate towards terrorists. They are completely mistaken – they are mistaken as to their religious teachings, they have a mistaken idea of freedom, and they are mistaken in what they want to achieve in life because they are inflicting suffering on others and also on

themselves. So they need compassion, they need understanding. Directing hatred and anger towards terrorists will not change or improve them. We need to bring transformation in them. For this we need patience, endurance, and compassion.

Q: How can we hope to positively educate a group like the terrorists, who are so overtly convinced that their way is the only way?
Sri Sri: They do not know that there are other traditions, which also claim to be the only way. Jesus said, 'I am the only way'. Krishna said, 'I am the goal, the only way'. The same is said in the Koran and in other scriptures. The purpose of these words is to bring a focus in human awareness, to bring up conviction in a particular moment, to reaffirm one's faith and practices. But these words have been mistaken to be a general statement meaning that this is the only way, to the exclusion of all other paths. They do not say, 'Absolutely, this is the only truth that exists', but rather, 'Right now, this is the path'. This wrong understanding of the verses of scripture has caused upheaval in the minds of many people and is used to justify narrow-mindedness. That is why, again and again, I say we need to emphasize on educating people in all the holy scriptures of the world. Each individual, especially every spiritual and religious leader, should be familiar with all other scriptures and traditions and schools of knowledge in the world.

You accept food and music from every part of the world without reservation, don't you? You don't have to be Danish to eat Danish pastries or Italian to eat pasta and pizzas. You don't have to be a German to enjoy Beethoven or an Indian to listen to sitar music. Why then, when it comes to wisdom, do we become so narrow-minded? The world would be a poorer place for not knowing the teachings of Buddha who said so much on consciousness and meditation. The world would be a poorer place for not knowing the wisdom of the Upanishads or Jesus' teachings on love or the words of Mohammed and Lao Tzu. When we think that only our own scripture holds truth, then we are nurturing fanaticism.

Terrorists have very narrow vision. What is needed is broader vision and deeper roots. This could bring about harmony and a non-violent attitude in all people. The only way to get rid of fanaticism in the world is broad-based education – multicultural, multireligious education – so that a child growing up does not think that only the Bible or only the Koran holds the truth. Broaden your vision; expand your horizon when it concerns wisdom, faith, and education in religious studies. That broader perspective will put an end to the growing fanaticism in the world today.

Q: Your position is that the key response to the situation in the world today is to educate people in human values, and until we have done that in all corners of the world, you say we will not be safe. Is that an achievable goal?

Sri Sri: Definitely! Until a few hundred years ago, there were tribal people who did not wear clothes. Today, in the most remote parts of the world, people wear clothes. People have been educated in understanding numbers, in using electricity, in using a telephone. All the people in the world have been educated in these things. If we can teach people how to count, we can teach them how to live. It is definitely possible. Educating people in human values is not a difficult thing because the values are already present. They are our nature. By nature we are friendly, cooperative, compassionate. If we are unfriendly, it is because of stress and tension. There are meditation and breathing techniques, which can be practised to reduce stress.

Q: What then are the practical steps we can take to lift up human values in the world?
Sri Sri: If a person identifies himself with a race, religion, culture or nationality, that's it! He remains in that position and he will fight for that and die for that and others will die with him. Instead, give him a broader perspective. First and foremost we are part of the Divine. Our second identity is that we are human beings. The third identity we have is that we are male or female. The fourth identity is that we belong to a particular nation. The fifth identity is that we belong to a particular religion. If the right order of identity is understood, then human values are honoured. But if I identify myself with a religion or nationality, forgetting that first I am part of the Divine and that I am a human being, then I bring misery onto myself and onto others also.

Q: If you had the ear of the whole world for one minute, what would your message be?
Sri Sri: Life is sacred. Celebrate life. Care for others and share whatever you have with those less fortunate than you. Broaden your vision, for the whole world belongs to you.

Religions

Religion has three aspects: value, ritual, and symbol. The moral and spiritual values are common to all traditions. The symbols and practices, those rituals and customs that form a way of life within a religion, are what distinguish one tradition from another and give each one its charm. The symbols and practices are like the banana skin, and the spiritual values – the quest for truth and knowing deep within us that we are part of divinity – are the banana. People in every tradition have thrown away the banana and are holding onto the skin.

This distinction [among] value, ritual, and symbol was made in ancient times. The Sanskrit term 'smriti' refers to those practices that are appropriate to a time and place, those things that are time-bound. 'Shruti' refers to those values which are timeless. And in the right order of things, what is time-bound is secondary to what is timeless or eternal. Putting religious concepts before human values creates havoc. In all traditions, we find the order inverted. People tend to hold what is time-bound – the symbols and practices, those things which give them an individual identity – before the values. Then fanaticism flourishes and the differences have to be defended.

We can see this today in the wars taking place around the world in the name of religion. If we could focus on the values, the larger truth that the symbol represents, then most of the conflict in the world will be resolved.

Symbols vary between religions because they have to do with the relative factors of location, environment, and time. The crescent moon and star on the flag of Islam were chosen by people living in a desert region where evening is a pleasant relief from the scorching heat of the day. The sun was chosen as a religious symbol in Japan and in Tibet where it gives welcome warmth and a feeling of elevation. Symbols are relative, but they are intended to lead us to something beyond the symbol, to the essence of religion. We need to reach for the deeper value, not to be stopped by the apparent difference. Practices are also time-bound – how you should dress, what name you are to take, what you can eat, how many wives you may have, how persons should be punished if they make some mistake. In all traditions you find practices like these that were necessary at the time that they were instituted, but they may no longer serve a good purpose today. In the Koran, it is prescribed that if someone steals, their hand must be cut off. At one time, a Christian who wanted to be religious had to take a vow of poverty. Jains were not allowed to touch money – this was solved by having someone accompany them to carry their money for them. Jews could not work on the day of the Sabbath. For those who follow this rule today, it means they cannot turn on a light switch.

Fanaticism flourishes when religious concepts are put before human values. In returning to the values, we will see that much of the misery that has come into the world in the name of religion can be avoided. This identification of values does not require guilt and fear to be introduced. You will find guilt and fear used for control in the history of all the religious systems in the world, but such discipline is not needed today. At this time we need only to cultivate love and understanding. The timeless values are a deep caring for all life, a responsible attitude towards the planet, non-violence, compassion and love, friendliness and cooperation, generosity and sharing, integrity, honesty and sincerity, moderation in one's activity, service, commitment and responsibility, peace, contentment, enthusiasm. These values are the very foundation of social order, justice, and progress. Human values are social and ethical norms common to all cultures and societies, as well as religions. They represent a melding of social progress and spiritual growth.

Within the religious fanaticism that has grown in the world, you will find a basic lack of understanding of other religions. A comprehensive study of various religions would support the broader view that one supreme and caring intelligence has expressed itself to different people at different times and in different ways. Fanaticism comes to people who feel insecure. This broader view gives a sense of belonging while still allowing people to be well founded in their own tradition.

There are ten major religions in the world, six from the Far East and four from the Middle East. In the Far East, Hinduism is the oldest. Then came Buddhism, Jainism, Taoism, Shintoism, and Sikhism. From the Middle East, Zoroastrianism is the oldest, and then came Judaism, Christianity, and Islam. Three of the Middle Eastern religions are rooted in the Old Testament: Islam, Christianity, and Judaism. In the Far East Shintoism and Taoism have completely separate sources. Buddhism, Jainism, and Sikhism have roots in Hinduism.

Far Eastern religions with different backgrounds peacefully coexist; Middle Eastern religions with a common root have conflicts. The six religions of the Far East have peacefully coexisted and intermingled over the centuries. Buddhism and Taoism have so completely accepted each other that you can find statues of Buddha in Taoist temples. Hinduism accepts Jain and Buddhist thought. Contrarily, the religions of the Middle East with a common root have warred with each other. The brothers of the same house fight while friends live with each other in a coherent manner. When I was in Japan I met several Shinto priests and Buddhist monks. They told me a story of travelling with President [George] Bush of

America. He asked a Shinto priest what the population of Shintoists in Japan was. The priest said, '80 per cent'. And he asked a Buddhist monk what the percentage of Buddhists was and the monk said, '80 per cent'. President Bush said, 'How could that be possible?' And they said, 'It is possible! Buddhists go to Buddhist temples and Shinto temples and Shintoists also go to Buddhist temples and Shinto temples.' In this story, we have a healthy model of cultures maintaining their identity and at the same time interacting with each other. We can find a similar model in India also. Within one family you will find Jains and Hindus and Sikhs. Individuals are free to choose whatever representation of Divinity they wish. They are not expected to adhere to the choice of the father or mother. This coexistence can happen when we put values first and symbols and practices second. Sometimes unexpected interconnections between religions are found.

If we look at the practices in Hinduism and Christianity, we see that Christianity is a bridge between Eastern Hinduism and Judaism. Many Roman Catholic practices found in the Hindu tradition are not found in Judaism, the root of Christianity. The use of beads is one example. Beads, called 'japamala', are a part of Hinduism, Buddhism, Sikhism, and Jainism. Catholics use rosary beads, but Judaism makes no use of beads. Another example is the use of incense, an ancient tradition found in the Hindu tradition and in Buddhism, Shintoism, Taoism as well as the Catholic Church. There are other links: the use of bells, worship of the feminine representation of God, the presence of multiple altars and icons in both Hindu temples and Catholic cathedrals, food as a part of ritual, marking the forehead with ash, the keeping of holy water in churches and temples, and more.

Christianity is a bridge between Eastern and Western traditions. When we feel conflict between our own religion and others, it may be because we are holding on to the wrong thing. If I say, 'Buddha is great', not simply because he is, but because I am a Buddhist, because I have a personal ego identification with the greatness of Buddha, then conflict arises. This ego identification with one's own tradition is a block to valuing other traditions. It leads to 'My God is better than your God' way of thinking. Humans have a strong need for an identification – the need to be 'someone' is part of our human nature. People will kill in order to preserve an identification they have made. We see this in the children in the United States who belong to gangs. They will kill to preserve the identity and the sense of belonging that they gain from gang membership. We need to see that our highest identity is not that of denomination or nationality – or gender or culture or profession or group membership. First we are part of Divinity and secondly we are human beings and part of the human family. This identification can free future generations of religious fanaticism.

There are certain texts in the scriptures of every tradition that, when narrowly interpreted or misinterpreted, cause misunderstanding and problems. In the Christian gospel, Jesus says, 'I am the only way. No one comes to the Father except through me.' This statement is widely taken by Christians to mean that you cannot attain the Kingdom of Heaven unless you believe in Jesus. But Krishna and Buddha have also made such statements: 'Come to me and me alone. I am the only way.' How can we understand the seeming contradiction in the fact that the founders of three major traditions each have claimed that they are the only way? We need to step back and look at these statements from a different angle. There is one eternal and omnipotent God who is not limited in the way His truth has been expressed throughout the ages. The one Consciousness that created the world has enormous intelligence and caring for the world. It brings up whatever is needed at the time that it is needed. Can we think that God was not there for all people through all time? Can we limit the scope and mercy of God in this way? Another way to look at these 'I am the only way' statements is that Jesus, Krishna, and Buddha were saying the abstract cannot be approached directly, but only through the personal. The teacher, the enlightened one, comes to be a bridge for you so that you can move from that which you can see and know to that which is invisible and unknown, from that which is changing and impermanent to that which is imperishable.

There is one eternal and omnipotent God who is not limited in the way His truth has been expressed. Saying 'I am the only way' is also a means of focusing attention. In every religion, there are words offered which bring this focus. Jesus said, 'Those who have come before me are robbers and thieves.' He meant, 'You are thinking about the prophets who came before me and ignoring what is present. The prophets are stealing your minds and attention. I am here now. Come to me and me alone. Don't look anywhere else.' Krishna has spoken in this way also: 'Look only here. I am the only one.' And Buddha said, 'I am the past, the present, and the future. I come again and again in every age.' The eternal Son of God has come more than once – He has manifested many times. In the guru's great generosity he returns again and again, bringing wisdom from age to age. We have many conflicting scriptural statements between religions and we also find contradictory scripture[s] within each religion. As an example, Jesus is described as the only Son of God, but then instructs his followers to pray, 'Our father in heaven.' Is there one son or many sons? These things need to be looked into.

'I am the only way' means the teacher comes to be a bridge so that you can move from what is known to what is unknown. We hear that we need to be tolerant of other religions, but I say we shouldn't be tolerant. Tolerance means that you don't like something, but you will put up with it. Respect is a better word. Respectfulness is a quality of divine consciousness. When someone respects you, it is their generosity speaking, not your virtue. When you respect someone, it is a sign of your magnanimity. How much respect you give to people is a sign of your own value. When we find the commonality in all religions, then respect will come. Then we can peacefully coexist and build a harmonious environment. Every major tradition has made a contribution to wisdom. The message of love and service in Christianity is unparalleled. The message of meditation and the theory of mindfulness in Buddhism are immeasurably profound. The knowledge of universe and self and life in the Vedic tradition is unmatched. The theory of karma is without equal in the Jain tradition. It is not necessary to see one tradition as better than another. All the religions of the world belong to all the world's people. The Divine has brought forth knowledge in different parts of the world at different times. Each of us belongs to the Divine and can claim all that the Divine has given as our own.

Every major tradition has made a contribution to wisdom. Read the sacred scriptures of any tradition and see them from a new angle. They all lead you to the basic human values of love, compassion, and joy. You will find no religion that does not advocate truth, peace, service, compassion, and caring for life.

Q: What does it mean to be enlightened?
Sri Sri: Enlightenment is like a joke! It's like a fish searching for the ocean. Once upon a time, there was a congregation of fishes who got together to discuss who had seen the ocean. None of them could actually say they had seen the ocean. Then, one fish said, 'I think my great-grandfather had seen the ocean!' A second fish said, 'Yes, yes. I also heard about this.' A third fish said, 'Yes, certainly, his great-grandfather had seen the ocean.' So they built a huge temple and made a statue of the great-grandfather of that particular fish. They said, 'He had seen the ocean. He had been connected with the ocean.'

Enlightenment is the very core of our being; going into the core of our self and living our life from there. We all came into this world gifted with innocence, but gradually, as we became more intelligent, we lost our innocence. We were born with silence, and as we grew up, we lost the silence and were filled with words. We lived in our hearts, and as time passed, we moved into our heads. Now the reversal of this journey is enlightenment. It is the journey from head back to the heart, from words back to silence; getting back to our innocence in spite of our intelligence. Although very simple, this is a great achievement. Knowledge should lead you to that beautiful point of 'I don't know'.

The completion of knowledge will lead you to amazement and wonder. It makes you aware of this existence. Mysteries are to be lived, not understood. One can live life so fully in its completeness, in its totality. Enlightenment is that state of being that is mature and unshakable by any circumstance. Come what may, nothing can rob the smile from your heart. Not identifying with limited boundaries and feeling 'all that exists in this universe belongs to me', this is enlightenment. Enlightenment is a state of being so mature as to be unshakable by any circumstance.

Un-enlightenment is easy to define. It is limiting yourself by saying, 'I belong to this particular place', or 'I am from that culture'. It's like children saying, 'My dad is better than your dad', or 'My toy is better than your toy'. I think most people around the world are stuck in that mental age group. Just the toys have changed. Adults say, 'My country is better than your country.' A Christian will say, 'The Bible is truth,' and a Hindu will say, 'The Vedas are truth. They are very ancient.' Muslims will say, 'The Koran is the last word on God.' We attribute glory to something just because we are from that culture, not for what it is. If one could take credit for all that exists throughout the ages and feel as though 'it belongs to me', then that is maturity. 'This is my wealth because I belong to the Divine.'

The Divine, according to time and space, gave different knowledge in different places. One becomes the knower of the whole universe and sees that, 'all the beautiful flowers are all from my garden'. The whole evolution of man is from being somebody to being nobody, and from being nobody to being everybody. Have you observed that young children have that sense of belonging, that oneness, that innocence? As we grow up we lose that innocence and become more cunning. The innocence of an ignorant man has no value, and the cunning of an intelligent man also has no value. Enlightenment is a rare combination of innocence and intelligence, with words to express and, at the same time, being very silent. In that state, the mind is fully in the present moment. Whatever is necessary is revealed to you in a natural and spontaneous way. You just sit and the song flows through you.

Q: Is enlightenment really possible for the average person?
Sri Sri: The answer is: 'Yes, a big YES.' Enlightenment is definitely possible for the ordinary individual. Actually, it is easier than for someone who thinks that [he or she is] special. You see, when someone thinks [he or she is] special [his or her] ego becomes involved. 'I am a great teacher or I am a great writer,' that is only ego. The ego wants to be special and this may cause someone to get stuck for a long time. Whenever someone is ordinary, simple, innocent, and natural, that is enlightenment. Enlightenment is your very nature. It is in you already, in the form of a seed. When you drop all the tensions and hang-ups and become natural, then it is right in your hand. We simply need to let go of the old patterns that are in the mind, just drop them. Then you see that something in you flowers and dawns. It is so beautiful. In my teachings there is a lot of focus on the breath because our breath plays a very important role. The breath is the connecting link between the inner world of the mind and the outer world of body and environment. You see, there are seven levels of existence: body, breath, mind, intellect, memory, ego, and Being. Meditation works by bringing an effect from the level of Being to the mind. With the breath we bring this effect to the physical level as well.

You see, there is a rhythm in nature. Seasons come and go. Everything in life has a particular pattern and order. In your own body, there is a rhythm, too. You feel hungry at a certain time and sleepy at a certain time. The body has a particular rhythm. Life has a particular rhythm. Similarly, your breath also goes in a particular pattern. Your emotions move in a particular rhythm, as well as your thoughts. All these rhythms arise from your Being, which has its own rhythm.

In Sudarshan Kriya, we get into the rhythm of our Being and see how Being is permeating our emotions, our thoughts, our breath, and our bodies. In a very short amount of time, every cell of the body becomes so alive and releases all the toxins and negative emotions it has stored from times past. Once again, we are able to smile from our hearts. It is very precious knowledge.

People who are trying to be what they are not become unnatural and create much more tension and stress. That is why one must go deep into the source of their nature, their Being, and come from there. You see, I don't say that you will never get upset again in life. If someone promises you that you will never get upset ... it just is not true. You may still get upset, but the quality of your life will not be the same. You will not get so caught up in your emotions for long periods of time. People have found that after they do Sudarshan Kriya, they are able to come back to themselves very quickly. Whatever mood comes up, they are able to let go and come back and enjoy much, much more.

Chapter Thirteen

The Knowledge Sheets

Life energy, the consciousness has enormous potentialities, the power and the intelligence. It is this intelligence that knows, how tall each stem should be and where it shall be green or yellow, hard or soft. The seed has the whole structure of how the plant will develop.

Guruji does not read at all. Once he himself had said that he could not read more than two pages of any book as he either went into meditation or fell asleep! On the other hand, he can, at the drop of a hat, give a talk on any topic and come out with such profound gems of wisdom, framed in the simplest terms, that they are accessible to anyone. Out of these impromptu talks with disciples were born, a few years ago, what are now known as 'knowledge sheets', which basically consist of aphorisms, or condensed knowledge, on a particular topic. I have always found it fascinating to watch Guruji formulating a knowledge sheet. It is usually a Wednesday late afternoon or evening, when he sits with a group of people and answers their queries on any one subject, which makes up the knowledge sheet. These knowledge sheets are so unique that even though the subject is of a serious nature, the atmosphere is one of lightness and hilarity. In such simple words and with such eloquence, a short knowledge sheet is born, which is then faxed or emailed to more than 4000 satsang centres around the world where it is read. The demand for such knowledge sheets has increased so much that they are now available on the Internet, and some newspapers in India and Europe have also started publishing them regularly. I am including here some of the knowledge sheets taken from the books *An Intimate Note to the Sincere Seeker* and *Celebrating Silence.*

Don't label yourself

Right away, stop judging yourself and labelling yourself and your expression of love.

You are clearly like a ripe fruit. We assume the Divine qualities and we do not analyse or cultivate them.

Love finds its expression spontaneously

When the mango is ripe its colour changes and you can spot it ... at a distance.

Being in utter love

Being in utter love inspires. It brings confidence in applying knowledge. The visible sign of utter love is an undying smile.

The Self knows neither sorrow nor death, yet in it flow all the relative events.

It is easy to be detached when you are not in love. Being in utter love, and yet undisturbed, caring yet not worried, persistent yet not perturbed, are all the obvious signs of the Self shining through.

Hide your dispassion and express your love.

By expressing your dispassion, you lose enthusiasm in life.

And by not expressing love you feel stifled.

Expressing dispassion may bring ego.

Hide dispassion in your heart like the roots of a tree.

A love that withstands rejection will be free from anger and ego.

A commitment that withstands humiliation will be one-pointed and reach its goal.

Wisdom that withstands emotional turbulence will get integrated in life.

Faith that withstands a million chances of doubt will bring perfection.

Events that withstand Time become morals for millions.

What is the purpose of love?

Love in itself is the end not the means to something. A purpose is always related to something that has an end. The purpose of cooking is to eat. The purpose of comfort is to live. A tree blossoms, what is the purpose? Love itself is the end.

The purpose of everything is to be in love. The Guru is love. The Guru kindles such an unusual love, beyond fear, anxiety, hatred, greed, jealousy. Love that encompasses the whole universe.

What is the purpose of love?

The question itself is irrelevant.

Desire

All desires are for happiness. That is the goal of desire, isn't it? But how often does your desire lead you to the goal? Have you thought about the nature of desire? It simply means joy tomorrow and not now.

Joy is never tomorrow. It is always now.

How can you really be joyful right now when you have desires?

Desire appears to lead you to happiness, but in fact it cannot. That is why desire is maya (illusion).

Ego

When is there ego?

1. When you don't get attention.
2. When you seem to be losing attention.
3. When you get attention.

Ego causes heaviness, discomfort, fear, anxiety. Ego does not let love flow. Ego is separateness, non-belongingness, wanting to prove and possess. Ego can be transcended by knowing the Truth, by enquiring 'Who am I?' Often, you feel contempt or jealousy towards someone who is egoistical. But rather you should have compassion or even pity.

There is also a positive aspect of ego. Ego drives you to do work. A person will do a job either out of compassion or out of ego. Most of the work in society is done out of ego. But in satsang work is done out of love. When you wake up and see that there is nothing to be proved and nothing to possess, ego dissolves.

Judgements and good company

Though you have heard 'don't judge', judgement comes unavoidably in day-to-day life. By the actions and behaviours of people, you either approve or disapprove [of them].

But always remember that everything is changing, and do not hold on to the judgement, otherwise it gets solidified like a rock. It brings misery for you and for others.

If judgements are lighter, like air, like a breeze, they bring in fragrance and then move away. Or they could bring a foul smell, then move away. But they should not stay forever.

Judgements are so subtle that you are not even aware of their existence. Judging or labelling someone as judgemental is also a judgement. Only in the state of Being when you are full of love and compassion, can you ever be free from all judgements.

Yet the world cannot move without judgements. Until you judge something as good or bad you cannot do any action. If you see rotten apples in the market, you say, 'no good'. It is only the good ones that you will buy. If someone lies to you ten times, you think the next time he speaks it could also be a lie. A judgement happens automatically.

See the possibility that people and things can change at any time and don't hold on to judgement.

You need to judge your company. Your company can pull you up or pull you down. The company that drags you down towards doubt, dejection, blame, complaints, anger, delusion, and desires is bad company. The company that pulls you towards joy, enthusiasm, service, love, trust, and knowledge is good company.

When someone complains, first you listen, then you nod, then you sympathize, then you complain.

The purpose of life

Our first and foremost commitment in the world is to do seva or service.

If there is fear or confusion in your life it is because you lack commitment.

The very thought 'I am here in this world to do seva', dissolves the 'I' and when the 'I' dissolves, worries dissolve. Seva is not something you do out of convenience or for pleasure. The ultimate purpose of life is to be of service.

An uncommitted mind is miserable. A committed mind may experience rough weather but will reap the fruits of its toil.

When you make service the sole purpose in life, it eliminates fear, brings focus in your mind and purposefulness, action and long-term joy ... and maybe short-term problems!

Success

Q: How was yesterday's programme? Was it successful?
Sri Sri: There is no question of success if you have nothing to gain. There is nothing to gain if you have only come to give and serve. Success indicates non-supremacy. Success means what? It indicates that there are chances of failure. If something is supreme, there is nothing to lose. People running after success only exhibit their limitations.

Success means crossing a limit. To cross a limit you have to assume that you have a limit. Assuming a limit is underestimating yourself. If you have no boundaries, then where is your success? If you have limitless access, then there is no success. You don't say that you successfully drank a glass of water, because it is well within your capabilities. But when you do something that is beyond your perceived limits, you claim success.

When you realize your boundlessness, then no action is an achievement.

Anyone who claims to be successful only reveals his limitation. If you feel very successful, it means that you have underestimated yourself. All your gains can be smaller than you. Taking pride in any gains is belittling yourself.
Sheila: What if you feel that you are not serving successfully?
Sri Sri: When you serve others, you may feel that you have

not done enough, but you will not feel that you have been unsuccessful. Real service is when you feel that you have not done enough.

Kai: You are not very successful! (Laughter)

Sri Sri: I am just full!

Religion and politics

The role of religion is to make one righteous and loving, and politics means caring for people and their welfare. When religion and politics don't coexist, then you have corrupt politicians and pseudo-religious leaders.

A religious man who is righteous and loving will definitely [take] care of the welfare of the whole population and hence become a true politician. And for a true politician to be righteous and loving he cannot but be religious. All the avatars and prophets have been caring for people and so were in politics. You can find many examples to this effect.

When religions restrict the freedom to worship and restrict modes of worship, they become unsuitable for creating a harmonious society. When religion becomes all-encompassing and gives full freedom to pray and worship in any manner – that religion will bring righteousness and peace in people and will be suitable for any society. People think politics and religion have to be kept separate because many religions did not give freedom to worship and did not care for all people equally. History has shown that religion has created conflict but irreligious societies (e.g., communism) have created chaos and corruption.

Today, both religion and politics need reform. Religion has to become broader and more spiritual to allow freedom of worship and broader to encompass all the wisdom in the world.

And politicians have to become more righteous and spiritual.

Karma

Some karma can be changed and some cannot.

When you prepare a dessert, if there is too little sugar or too little butter, too much or too little milk, it can all be adjusted, repaired. But once it is cooked, it cannot be reversed.

If buttermilk is sour, milk or salt can be added to make it drinkable but it can never be reversed back to milk.

Prarabdha karma (the karma that forms one's present body and life) cannot be changed. Sanchita karma (the sum of one's past karmas) can be changed by spiritual practices. Satsang burns the seed of all negative karma.

When you praise someone, you take on their good karma.

When you blame someone, you take on their bad karma.

Know this and surrender both good and bad karma to the Divine and be free.

Do it until you become it

Virtues have to be practised until they become your nature. Friendliness, compassion, and meditation should continue as practices until you realize that they are your very nature.

The flaw in doing something as an act is that you look for a result. When it is done as your nature you are not attached to the result and you continue doing it.

An action that arises from your nature is neither tiring nor frustrating. For example, daily routines like brushing your teeth are not even considered actions because they are so integrated into your life. You do all this with 'doership'. When seva is made part of your nature it happens without 'doership'.

Q: When do you realize that compassion, seva, and meditation are your nature?

Sri Sri: When you cannot be without them.

Wise men continue their practices just to set an example even though for them there is no need for any practices.

Faith is your wealth

If you think your faith in God is doing a favour to God, then you are mistaken. Your faith in God or Guru does nothing to God or Guru. Faith is your wealth.

Faith gives you strength instantly. Faith brings you stability, centredness, calmness, and love. Faith is your blessing.

If you lack faith, you will have to pray for faith. But to pray, you need faith! This is a paradox.

People put their faith in the world, but the whole world is just a soap bubble. People have faith in themselves, but they don't know who they are. People think they have faith in God, but they really do not know who God is.

There are three types of faith:

1. Faith in yourself: Without faith in yourself, you think, 'I can't do this: this is not for me: I will never be liberated in this life.'
2. Faith in the world: You must have faith in the world or you can't move an inch. You deposit money in the bank with faith that it will be returned. If you doubt everything, nothing will happen for you.
3. Faith in the Divine: Have faith in the Divine and you will evolve.

All these faiths are connected; you must have all three for each to be strong. If you start doubting in one, you will begin to doubt everything.

Bill: Atheists have faith in themselves and faith in the world, but not in God.

Sri Sri: Then they don't have complete faith in themselves – and their faith in the world cannot be constant because there are always changes. Lack of faith in God, the world, or yourself brings fear.

Faith makes you full – faithful!

Q: Is there a pure atheist?
Sri Sri: A pure atheist is impossible to find. An atheist is one who does not believe in anything that is not concrete and tangible. Life is not all concrete and tangible. Nor is the universe. Whether it is business, science or art, they all involve a certain amount of guesswork, assumptions, imagination, and intuition. All of them are ethereal in nature and are not tangible. The moment an atheist accepts, even remotely, a field that is unexplainable, he ceases to be an atheist. Any intelligent person cannot rule out the mystery in life and the universe and hence cannot honestly be an atheist! The so-called atheists are perhaps only denouncing certain concepts of God.

Q: Was Buddha an atheist?
Sri Sri: No in one sense because he professed emptiness, which is very hard for an atheist to accept and yes in another sense because he did not profess concepts of God.

Jim: An atheist believes only what he can see but Buddha said all that you see is not real.

Sri Sri: If only in the present day atheists could be Buddhas ...

Chapter Fourteen

A Glimpse into Eternity

In the company of your friend, you lose your centredness. Your enemy puts you back in yourself. Your friend sympathizes with you and makes you believe in matter. Your enemy makes you feel helpless and takes you to the spirit. So your enemy is your friend and your friend is your enemy. Krishna said to Arjuna, "One who is unfriendly everywhere — including to himself — his consciousness is stable and his awareness is established."

It was winter and the ghats (a ghat is a broad flight of steps leading down to the bank of a river in India, generally used by bathers and worshippers) were deserted. There was no moonrise at this time. Only a tiny crescent was visible on the horizon: Shiva's moon. Seven years later, on a cold misty December night, we were once again on the Ganges in a boat with Guruji. In the distance, one could barely distinguish the outline of the ghats and the lights of Varanasi shimmering in the dark, like little oil lamps. The atmosphere was magical as ever; again, someone started singing softly a bhajan and again Sri Sri closed his eyes, a mysterious smile on his face. Once more my soul soared high – but this time I knew where I was going: there, behind my heart, to a tiny point of warmth and light, of concentration and delight.

I looked back on the years that had elapsed since my first ride on the Ganges of Life with Guruji. I had spent innumerable days with him, listened to him for hours, meditated with him, talked to him, and travelled with him all over India. Teaching his Basic Course has been an enlightening experience, a boon, and an honour. Time has flown; yet it has stood still. I have changed, but something in me, which is eternal, has remained the same: the same François, the same secret 'I', unchanged at ten years of age, or fifty, or even eighty; the same 'I' which passes from one life to another. A touch of Guruji has put me in touch with my Self. After all these years, I have finally come to understand that we are all born with this innocence and love.

Yet the mystery – who is Sri Sri – has deepened over the years. Many people have strong certitudes: 'He is Krishna', say some; 'Shiva', think others; 'an Avatar', I have heard others say. Yet for me, the nearest to truth would be to state that Sri Sri is an embodiment of Love. He is what we all really are, just more obvious. Coming near him is like being embraced in a cocoon of love, watching him always triggers love, being with him is being swept away by love, looking at him is feeling love for everyone. As he himself has said so many times: 'Love is present in all creation. Everything is Love. But you have never related it in your life other than by name and form.'

Suffice it to say that Sri Sri is a glimpse into eternity, a window to our inner Self; he is the smile that we all secretly carry in ourselves. He has come to take us from the religious to the spiritual, from fear to the innocence that has always been in us.

Come, sit in this boat and let it carry you to the other side. In joy and celebration.

Appendix 1

The Courses

As I grew in AOL, I quickly discovered that the Art of Living is a foundation that has centres in more than 130 countries and offers a variety of courses. Here is a sample of the infinite variety of courses that Sri Sri has devised.

Courses for Children

The world belongs to children; they are the ones who are going to shape the twenty-first century. Guruji has bestowed utmost attention to the future generations and has the knack of teaching profound things in a playful manner.

Namrita remembers arriving at the Bangalore ashram after a long and tiring bus journey from Pondicherry. She recounts: 'It felt so good to be welcomed by all these smiling bright faces and after registering I was told to go for lunch. Walking towards the kitchen, I heard an ancient prayer being chanted by children in their young melodious voices and my feet hurried me towards this sound. I suddenly felt my tiredness fall away. Reaching there I grabbed hold of the first person I saw as I had to know who these children were and what they were doing! I was so drawn to these kids with their bubbling joy and tinkling laughter, who looked so different from the children I was used to seeing in the cities! I was told that all these kids were taking part in a camp called ART Excel. What was this camp was the next question that sprang up in my mind and, lunch forgotten, I started talking to the teacher about what this programme was all about. Dinesh [an ashramite] explained: This ART Excel (All Round Training in Excellence) programme is a course specifically designed for youngsters. Today we [are seeing] how, all over the world, such a great percentage of teenagers are suffering from depression, drug addiction, and violence. The ART Excel programme presents practical tools to alleviate tension, increase their focus, and augment overall well-being. The 18-hour programme incorporates ancient Vedic knowledge within a practical framework that appeals to youth of all ethnic, racial, and religious backgrounds. The programme helps teenagers drop their inhibitions, lethargy, shyness, and unfriendliness. Teens develop a spirit of adventure, which enables them to deal with the unexpected twists and turns, upsets, and challenges life may bring. A typical weekend includes yoga postures, breathing techniques, meditation, and processes that reawaken the traditional value system of love, compassion, peace, generosity, gratitude, and grace. Another ART Excel teacher, Sharmila, feels that "hearts and minds are thus opened to the greater values of life. Teens leave happier, more self-aware, with an experience of mutual acceptance, sensitivity towards others, and tools that they can use every day to deal with their emotions".

'Translated into practical living this means that teens learn how to face their emotions and deal with them in positive and constructive ways, rather than blindly react to their environment. Techniques of profound relaxation enable teens to release stress caused by pressures at school and the demands of a tension-filled society. Once learned correctly, these techniques can be used in any place or situation to bring calmness, increase focus, and augment mental clarity. Teens often comment that they use the knowledge of breathing taught on the course to decrease exam anxiety and more easily recall their studies. Those who like to walk on the wilder side of life find an opportunity for self-reflection and moderation.

'I was very inspired and as time went on I became an ART Excel teacher and discovered for myself the magic of this course and how a shy child like Archana blossomed during the camp. Activities throughout the course are designed to lead the participants into a closer understanding of themselves and others. Those with low self-esteem gain self-confidence in this safe, stimulating, and nurturing setting. It is such a joy to watch them band together to help each other when someone is feeling depressed, angry or frustrated! Many a crisis has been averted just by having the loving support of peers.'

Corporate Courses

Today, stress has become a way of life in the corporate world, because of increasing pressures to achieve and produce at a faster rate. These high levels of stress, which are being experienced in the work place, regardless of one's earning capacity or status, create untold havoc on the functioning of the body and lead to blood pressure, heart problems, and even cancer. Unless the quality of life is improved, not only will disappointment and frustration continue to interfere with creativity, productivity, and harmonious interaction, affecting both business and personal life, but also the harm to the body will not be contained.

Five years ago we met Ajit, an executive with an MNC [multinational company], and our first impression was of a completely stressed-out person. He just could not relax and would fidget non-stop. Over the years, after doing the different courses, beginning with the Corporate Course, there has been such a vast improvement in him that he is an inspiration in [himself]!

The Self-Management Seminar is a proven method for improving the quality of life. It is a practical and effective training programme that can empower managers and employees to experience unshakable calmness and inner clarity in the midst of any challenge or crisis. Says Vinod Menon, one of the corporate AOL teachers: 'The Self-Management Seminar is based on innovative breathing techniques that permanently reduce stress and heighten one's mental clarity and awareness. These powerful techniques, which are easily learned and practised, improve concentration, enhance creativity, and increase efficiency.'

The techniques and processes taught during the seminar create fundamental changes in the lives of employees that are essential for transforming any work environment. The seminar also incorporates basic principles for effective living, emphasizing the essential human values that help individuals lead more fulfilling and productive lives. Ajit now teaches these courses that are customized to suit specific company needs and has seen people benefit in different ways, the most obvious being enhanced creativity and clarity of mind for executives and employees along with improved productivity and team efficiency. As stress gets reduced, he finds a greater commitment and job satisfaction in people who have attended the seminar. Many participants felt that their health improved and there was a general feeling of well-being along with increased physical energy, heightened enthusiasm, and enhanced self-esteem.

The Self-Management Seminar is divided into four sessions and can be held over a weekend or during the week. Even the aeronautical world has benefited from the Corporate Courses, as William Hayden, senior systems analyst, NASA, tells us: 'As an engineer I need to be both analytical and creative. Mental clarity and stamina are also essential. The Self-Management Seminar has given me the tools to enhance these abilities. An additional plus is a better sense of health and well-being.'

This seminar offers specific breathing techniques that infuse the body with energy and harmonize the natural rhythms of the body, mind, and emotions. Due to the intensity and stress of the business environment, these natural rhythms get distorted. Experienced as burnout or ill health, this discord creates fatigue in the body and mind, creating mental and emotional imbalances, lowering one's productivity and efficiency.

The Art of Living Course for Depression

Depression is a disabling disease that takes the joy out of life for millions around the world – men, women, and children

– regardless of race, income or family background. Depression also contributes to the downward spiral of emotions, leading to many diseases: from cancer and HIV to asthma and cardiovascular problems. Finding an effective treatment for depression is a global health concern. The Art of Living Course for Depression offers a variety of techniques that have been documented by independent medical studies to be effective in alleviating depression. These simple, yet powerful, techniques have advantages over many other forms of treatment because they are free from negative side-effects, cut healthcare costs, and are easy to learn and practise in daily life.

Due to the often long-term and chronic nature of depression, Art of Living Courses for Depression usually run longer than regular Art of Living courses and are sometimes taught as in-residence programmes. (See also Chapter 11.)

The Art of Living Course for Coronary Heart Disease

It is common belief that stressful life events lead to the risk of coronary heart disease (CHD). Anyone can develop CHD regardless of age, sex, race or ethnic background. Sometimes, there may be no warning signs or symptoms and even if there are any, either they are not noticed or they are ignored. The history of CHD is higher in the urban population than in rural population, which is a major cause for premature death.

As mentioned in Chapter 11, when three risk factors like hyperlipidaemia (high fat and cholesterol content in blood), hypertension, and smoking together afflict an individual, the chances of a heart attack are seven times higher, whereas the risk is twofold when these are individually present. Whatever the risk factor, the basic pathology of CHD is deposition of LDL cholesterol (harmful cholesterol), fat, and other substances on the walls of the coronary arteries. These deposits thicken the arterial walls and narrow the arteries, which slows down or blocks the flow of blood. The heart receives a constant supply of oxygen through blood; any blockage of the flow may result in chest pain (angina pectoris) and myocardial infarction (heart attack) or even death.

An individual can improve the quality of life by avoiding the things harmful for health and by accepting things that are good. Regular Sudarshan Kriya practice, as well as Ujjai, Pranayama, and Bhastrika can work wonders here.

Appendix 2

Table 1
Effect of Sudarshan Kriya Practice on LIPID Profile and LIPID Peroxidation in Normal Individuals

Group mg %	Total choles-terol (SD)[2]	TG[1] mg % Mean (SD)	HDLc mg % Mean (SD)	LDLc mg % Mean (SD)	VLDL[3] mg % Mean (SD)	MDA[4] (nmole/ml) Mean (SD)	p value
Before SKP	189.35 (37.89)	139.8 (73.78)	43.18 (7.16)	118.32 (37.92)	28 (14.81)	3.32 (1.27)	
7th day SKP	168.62 (28.94)	160.22 (86.41)	46.56 (7.84)	91.76 (31.10)	31.98 (17.34)	2.0 (0.7)	

[1]Triglyceride.
[2]Standard deviation.
[3]Very-low-density lipoprotein.
[4]Malondialdehyde.

Table 2
Effect of Sudarshan Kriya Practice on LIPID Profile and LIPID Peroxidation in Normal Individuals

Group mg %	Total choles- terol (SD)	TG mg % Mean (SD)	HDLc mg % Mean (SD)	LDLc mg % Mean (SD)	VLDL mg % Mean (SD)	MDA p value (nmole/ml) Mean (SD)
Before SKP	189.35 (37.89)	139.8 (73.78)	43.18 (7.16)	118.32 (37.92)	28 (14.81)	3.32 (1.27)
45th day	156.21	153.16	51.51	74.72	30.23	1.31
SKP	(26.33)	(73.71)	(7.73)	(26.52)	(14.78)	(0.38)

Total number of subjects: 46

References (Medical)

B. N. Gangadhar, N. Janakiramaiah, B. Sudarshan, and K. T. Shety, *Stress-related Biochemical Effects of Sudarshan Kriya Yoga in Depressed Patients*, National Institute of Mental Health and Neurosciences (NIMHANS), Bangalore, 1999.

B. L. Meti, *Effects of Sudarshan Kriya Practice on Auditory Middle Latency Responses*, Department of Neuro-physiology, NIMHANS, Bangalore, 1995.

N. Janakiramaiah, *Sudarshan Kriya and Heart Rate Variability*, Departments of Psychiatry and Neuro-physiology, NIMHANS, Bangalore, 1996.

B. L. Meti, T. R. Raju, N. Janakiramaiah, N. Venkatesh, P. J. Murthy, and B. N. Gangadhar, *Effects of Sudarshan Kriya in Dysthymic Disorders*, Departments of Neuro-physiology and Psychiatry, NIMHANS, Bangalore, 1996.

M. G. Harish, 'Treatment Effects of Sleep Pattern Abnormalities in Melancholic Depression', unpublished dissertation submitted to National Board of Examinations (Psychiatry), New Delhi, 1997.

D. Kovacic, 'The Art of Living Course for the Patients with Multiple Sclerosis: First Results', unpublished report to the Institute for Rehabilitation, the Republic of Slovenia, Ljubljana, 1999.

P. J. Naga Venkatesha Murthy, B. N. Gangadhar, N. Janakiramaiah, and D. K. Subhakrishna, 'Normalization of P300 Amplitude Following Treatment in Dysthymia', *Biological Psychiatry*, Vol. 42, 1997, pp. 740–43.

N. Janakiramaiah et al., 'Therapeutic Efficacy of Sudarshan Kriya Yoga (SKY) in Dysthymic Disorders', *NIMHANS Journal*, January 1998, pp. 21–28.

P. J. Naga Venkatesha Murthy et al., 'P300 Amplitude and Antidepressant Response to Sudarshan Kriya Yoga (SKY)', *Journal of Affective Disorders*, 1998, pp. 45–48.

B. L. Meti, T. R. Raju, N. Janakiramaiah, N. Venkatesh, P. J. Murthy, and B. N. Gangadhar, *Effects of Sudarshan Kriya in Dysthymic Disorders*, Departments of Neuro-physiology and Psychiatry, NIMHANS, Bangalore, 1996.

N. Janakiramaiah et al., 'Antidepressant Efficacy of Sudarshan Kriya Yoga (SKY) in Melancholia: A Randomized Comparison with ECT and Imipramine', *Journal of Affective Disorders*, Vol. 57, Issues 1-3, 2000, pp. 255–59.

M. Bhatia, A. Kumar, N. Bharadwaj, R. M. Pandey, and V. Kochupillai, *Electrophysiological Evaluation of Sudarshan Kriya: An EEG, BAER, P-300 Study*, All India Institute of Medical Sciences, New Delhi, 2001.